World Picture ATLAS

Holly Wallace

QED Publishing

Copyright © QED Publishing 2009
First published in the UK in 2009 by
QED Publishing
A Quarto Group Company
226 City Road
London EC1V 2TT

www.qed-publishing.co.uk

ISBN 978 1 84835 274 2

Printed and bound in Singapore

Author Holly Wallace
Consultants Clive Carpenter and
  Terry Jennings
Editor Eve Marleau
Designer Lisa Peacock
Cartography Red Lion

Publisher Steve Evans
Creative Director Zeta Davies
Managing Editor Amanda Askew

The words in *bold italic* are explained in the glossary on page 46.

Picture credits
Key: t=top, b=bottom, r=right, l=left, c=centre,
PP=People and Places, PR=Products and Resources,
PA=Plants and Animals

8–9 PP: Shutterstock 9tl Richard Welter, 9tr Maridav,
9c Konstantin Shevtsov, 9bl Jim Guy, 9bc Anson Hung,
9br Taylor Jackson **PR: Shutterstock** 9tl Petr Vaclavek,
9tr Tatiana Edrenkina, 9cl Dalibor, 9cr Jovan Nikolic, 9b
Lorraine Swanson **PA: Shutterstock** 8tl Mike Tan C.T,
8tc psamtik, 8tr Atlaspix, 8bl Scarabaeus, 8bc Chas, 8br
Viacheslav V. Fedorov
10–11 PP: Shutterstock 11tl Mike Norton, 11tc Sandra
van der Steen, 11tr Iofoto, 11cl Chee-Onn Leong, 11cr
IPK Photography, 11b Bhathaway **PR: Shutterstock** 11tl
ArchMan, 11tr Chepe Nicoli, 11cl MaszaS, 11cc Charles
T. Bennett, 11cr Nikola Bilicb, 11b Jovan Nikolic **PA:
Shutterstock** 10tl Steve Byland, 10tc Eric Isselée, 10tr
Ultrashock, 10bl Mighty Sequoia Studio, 10bc Kippy
Lanker, 10br
12–13 PP: Shutterstock 12t Jennifer Scheer, 12cl
Stuart Monk, 12cc Lisa F.Young, 12cr Albo, 12bl
Condor 36, 12br Rob Byron **PR: Shutterstock** 13tl
Gnuskin Petr, 13tc Jiri Vaclavek, 13tr Nikola Bilic, 13cl
Christopher Dodge, 13cr Anat-oli, 13b Heidi Brand
PA: Shutterstock 13tl James Pierce, 13tc Gabor Ruff,
13tr A Cotton Photo, 13bl Goldenangel, 13bc R, 13br
Mike Truchon
14–15 PP: Corbis 15cl Roger Ressmeyer **Shutterstock**
15t RJ Lerich, 15ccl Scott Kapich, 15ccr RJ Lerich, 15cr
Timothy Lee Lantgen, 15b Slazdi **PR: Shutterstock** 15tl
Ahnhuynh, 15tcl ShutterVision, 15tcr Provasilich, 15tr
Sean Gladwell, 15bl Marcel Jancovic, 15br Geoffrey
Kuchera **PA: Photoshot** 14tr NHPA/Lee Dalton
Shutterstock 14tl Joseph Galea, 14tc Vitaly Romanovich,
14cl Eric Isselée, 14bl Jaana Piira, 14br Eky Chan
16–17 PP: Alamy Images 16tl Peter Arnold Inc/
Arnold Newman, 16b Moodboard **Shutterstock**
16tc ATesevich, 16tr Guentermanaus, 16cr Ostill, 16cl
Grigory Kubatyan
PR: Shutterstock 17tl Matka Wariatka, 17tr Heidi
Brand, 17cl Ronald Sumners, 17cr Tatiana Edrenkina,
17bl Pavelr, 17br TsR **PA: Shutterstock** 17tl Karen
Givens, 17tr Urosr, 17cl Graeme Knox, 17cc ZTS, 17cr

Rubens Alarcon, 17b Eric Gevaert
18–19 PP: Shutterstock 18tl Urosr, 18tc Misha
Shiyanov, 18tr Pablo H Caridad, 18cl Mausinda, 18cr
Dan Breckwoldt, 18b Damian Gil **PR: Alamy Images**
19cr Arco Images GmbH **Photolibrary** 19tl National
Geographic **Shutterstock** 19tr Susan L. Pettitt, 19cl
Eric Isselée, 19cc ClimberJAK, 19b Eric Isselée **PA:
Shutterstock** 19tl Marcel Jancovic, 19tr CG-Art, 19cl
Filipe B.Varela, 19cc Nikola Bilic, 19cr Eric Isselée, 19b
Daniel Kirkegaard Mouritsen
20–21 PP: Alamy Images 21cl ZenZimage
Shutterstock 21tl Bond Girl, 21tr WitR, 21cc Eric
Gevaert, 21cr Aneta Skoczewska **PR: Shutterstock** 21tl
Heidi Brand,
21tr Pennyimages, 21cl Rui Vale de Sousa, 21cc
Fotohunter, 21cr Shira Raz, 21b Odelia Cohen **PA:
Dreamstime** 20tl **Shutterstock** 20tc Gert Johannes
Jacobus Vrey, 20tr Tezzstock, 20bl Christian Musat, 20bc
Bill Kennedy, 20br Arkady
22–23 PP: Shutterstock 23tl Ostill, 23tr Lukas
Hlavac, 23cl Alessio Ponti, 23cc Galyna Andrushko,
23cr Faberfoto, 23b Enote **PR: Alamy Images** 23tl
Blickwinkel
Shutterstock 23tr James Steidl, 23cl Nathalie Dulex,
23cc Riekephotos, 23cr Norman Chan, 23b Vinicius
Tupinamba **PA: FLPA** 22bl Michael & Patricia Fogden
Shutterstock 22tl Liga Alksne, 22tcl Eric Isselée, 22tcr
Victor Soares, 22tr Jenny Horne, 22br Helder Almeida
24–25 PP: Shutterstock 25t Stefanie van der Vinden,
25cl Michael Jung, 25cc PhotoSky 4t com, 25cr Sculpies,
25bl Pichugin Dmitry, 25br Lucian Coman
PR: Shutterstock 25tl Amfoto, 25tc Daniel Kirkegaard
Mouritsen, 25tr Teresa Azevedo, 25bl, 25bc Johnny
Lye, 25br Ahnhuynh **PA: Shutterstock** 24tl Graeme
Shannon, 24tr Johan Swanepoel, 24cl Mashe, 24cc Eric
Isselée, 24cr David Thyberg, 24b NREY
26–27 PP: Alamy Images 27tr Robert Harding Picture
Library Ltd **Getty Images** 27cr Denis Charlet/AFP
Shutterstock 27tl Joe Gough, 27cl Igor Kisselev, 27cb
Stephen Finn, 27b Stelian Ion **PR: Corbis** 26bl Niall
Benvie ©2004 The LEGO Group 27tr **Shutterstock**
27tl Tatiana Edrenkina, 27tr Tyler Olson, 27bc, 27br Falk
Kienas **PA: Shutterstock** 26tl Eric Isselée, 26tc Stephen
Finn, 26tr Keith Levit, 26cl HTuller, 26cr Thomas O'Neil,

26b 3355m
28–29 PP: Shutterstock 29tl Mary Lane, 29tc Vladimir
Sazonov, 29tr Nagy Melinda, 29cl Alexey Arkhipov, 29cr
Senai Aksoy, 29b Cristina Ciochina **PR: Shutterstock**
28tl Vladimir Chernyanskiy, 29tr János Németh, 28cl
Prono Filippo, 28cr Zuzule, 28bl Scodaru, 28br Tatarszkij
PA: Shutterstock 29tl Nikola Bilic, 29tr Gallimaufry,
29cl Sspopov, 29cr Dima Kalinin, 29bl Tund, 29br Yuliyan
Velchev
30–31 PP: Shutterstock 30tl Piotr Bieniecki, 30tc
PixAchi, 30tr Gueorgui Ianakiev, 30cl Sergey Kamshylin,
30cr Brykaylo Yuriy, 30b Brent Wong **PR: Shutterstock**
31tl Arteretum, 31tr Eric Isselée, 31cl Eric Isselée,
31cc Berit Ullmann, 31cr ARTSILENSEcom, 31b Steve
Noakes
PA: Getty Images 31tl De Agostini Picture Library
Shutterstock 31tr Ilker Canikligil, 31cl Alekcey, 31cc
Katja Kodba, 31cr Blazej Maksym, 31b Dinadesign
32–33 PP: Alamy Images 33b Bryan & Cherry
Alexander Photography **Shutterstock** 33tl Alexander
Chelmodeev,
33tc Denis Babenko, 33tr Dmitry Kosterev, 33cl
Scodaru, 33cr Tatiana Grozetskaya **PR: Rex Features**
33br **Shutterstock** 33tl Sergey Petrov, 33tc Elena
Schweitzer, 33tr Nicole Branan, 33bl Daniel G.Mata,
33bc Dalibor **PA: Shutterstock** 32tl Vladimir Melnik,
32tc Letty17, 32tr 3355m, 32bl Arnold John Labrentz,
32bc Tina Rencelj, 32br Eric Isselée
34–35 PP: Shutterstock 35tl Joseph Calev, 35tc
Markus Sevcik, 35tr Chubykin Arkady, 35cl Ayazad, 35cr
Connors Bros., 35b Vladyslav Byelov **PR: Getty Images**
35tl Lonely Planet Images/Patrick Syder **Shutterstock**
35tr Jovan Nikolic, 35cl Mircea Bezergheanu, 35cc
Johannsen, 35cr Arteretum, 35b Losevsky Pavel **PA:
Alamy Images** 34br Mike Lane **Shutterstock** 34tl
Armin Rose, 34tc John A. Anderson, 34tr Debra James,
34bl Debra James, 34bc Seleznev Oleg
36–37 PP: Shutterstock 36tl Pal Teravagimov,
36tr Chris Howey, 36cl Lebedinski Vladislav, 36cr
ARTEKI, 36cc Jeremy Richards, 36b 0399778584
PR: Shutterstock 37tl Robyn Mackenzie, 37tr Micha
Rosenwirth, 37cl Ygrek, 37cr Arteretum, 37bl Marc
Dietrich, 37br Norman Chan
PA: Shutterstock 37tl Thorsten Rust, 37tr Karen

Givens, 37cl Narcisa Floricica Buzlea, 37cc Benson HE,
37cr Irakite, 37b Vladimir Wrangel **38–39 PP: Alamy
Images** 39tr Mick Viet/Danita Delimont, 39tc Image
Broker **Shutterstock** 39tl Lakis Fourouklas, 39cl Vlad
Zharoff, 39cr David Wardhaugh, 39b Gusev Mikhail
Evgenievich **PR: Shutterstock** 39tl Olga Lyubkin, 39tc
Karen Winton, 39tr Joao Virissimo, 39bl A Schweitzer,
39br Jakub Kozák, 39bc Le Loft 1911 **PA: Istockphoto**
38br Chris Dascher Shutterstock 38tl Kkaplin, 38tr
Stanislav Khrapov, 38cl Craig Dingle, 38cr David Mckee,
38bl Jeff Carpenter
40–41 PP: Alamy Images 41cl Dennis Cox Shutterstock
41tl Tan Kian Khoon, 41tc Craig Hanson, 41tr
Mares Lucian, 41cr Holger Mette, 41b Freelion **PR:
Shutterstock** 41tl Norman Chan, 41tcl Gosper, 41tcr
Grzym, 41tr E.G.Pors, 41bl Robyn Mackenzie, 41br
Ivaschenko Roman **PA: Alamy Images** 40br Natural
Visions/Heather Angel **Shutterstock** 40tl Eric Gevaert,
40tc Dmitrijs Mihejevs, 40tr Eric Isselée, 40bl J. Norman
Reid, 40bc Shi Yali
42–43 PP: Alamy Images 43b David Wall
Shutterstock 43tl Jose Gil, 43tr Vera Bogaerts, 43cl
Brooke Whatnall, 43cc 4745052183, 43cr Midkhat
Izmaylov **PR: Shutterstock** 43tl Luis Francisco Cordero,
43tc RTimages, 43tr Mitzy, 43bl Marylooo, 43bc Michael
C. Gray, 43br Philip Lange **PA: Alamy Images** 42bc
Stephen Frink Collection **Shutterstock** 42tl Olga
Lyubkina, 42tc Jason Stitt, 42tr Susan Flashman, 42bl
Martin Horsky, 42br Mark R Higgins
44–45 PP: Alamy Images 44cl Mediacolor's
Shutterstock 44tl Viktor Gmyria, 44tr Chris Howey,
44cc Konstantin Shevtsov, 44cr Scott Kapich, 44b Armin
Rose **PR: Shutterstock** 45tl HelleM, 45tr Vera Bogaerts,
45cl Ramona Heim, 45cr Tonylady, 45bl Alex0001, 45br
Sam Chadwick **PA: Shutterstock** 44tl Nice_Pictures,
44tr Jan Martin Will, 44cl Ivan Histand, 44cr Gail
Johnson, 44bl Popovici Loan, 44br Andromed

Contents

How to use this atlas

Maps are drawings of what the Earth looks like from above. Maps show important features such as deserts, rivers and oceans, and how far apart countries are from each other in the world. A book of maps is called an *atlas*.

1 Title
This tells you which part of the world the map shows.

2 Locator globe
This shows where in the world the countries on the map are.

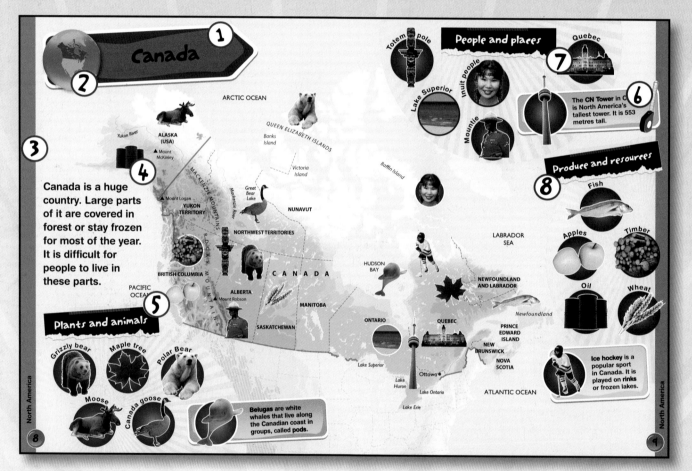

3 Side panel
This is the name of the *continent* that the countries on the map are in.

4 Picture
Every picture in the yellow bubbles is on the map. Can you find them all?

5 Plants and animals
Many different kinds of plants and animals live all over the world.

6 Scale
This means that this mountain, waterfall or building is shown on the *scale* on page 5.

7 People and places
The countries of the world and the people that live there can be different in many ways.

8 Produce and resources
Countries grow, make or use different things to make money.

What's on the map?

Maps use different kinds of writing and colours to show what is in each country. For example, a country name will look different to a river name. **Symbols** show features such as **capital cities**.

NORWAY Country name	CANARY ISLANDS Territory	Sonoran Desert Desert	AHAGGAR MOUNTAINS Mountain range
Country border	*Seram* Island	*Lake Vänern* Lake	ATLANTIC OCEAN Ocean
OHIO State	*ARU ISLANDS* Group of islands	*Missouri River* River	BAY OF BISCAY Small sea
State border	Berlin ● Capital city	▲ Mount Galdhøpiggen Mountain	Ice

Colour key

These colours show how high and how dry land is in different areas.

- more than 2000 metres
- 1500–2000 metres
- 1000–1500 metres
- 500–1000 metres
- 100–500 metres
- 0–100 metres

How high?

A scale can help to show the different sizes of mountains. If you see this symbol, come back to this page to see how big things really are.

The CN Tower is 553 metres tall. That's the height of 185 buses.

A bus is about 3 metres high.

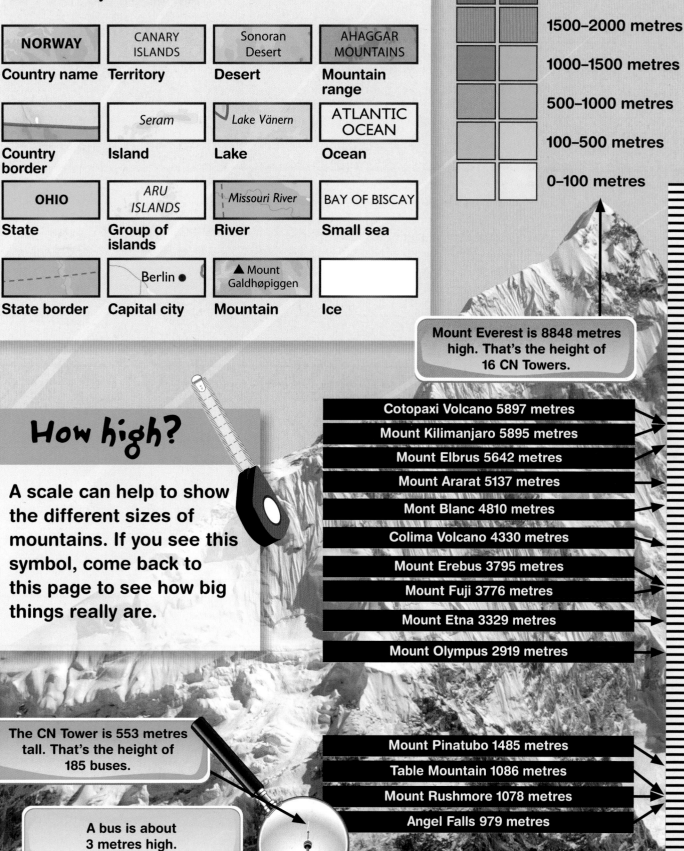

Mount Everest is 8848 metres high. That's the height of 16 CN Towers.

- Cotopaxi Volcano 5897 metres
- Mount Kilimanjaro 5895 metres
- Mount Elbrus 5642 metres
- Mount Ararat 5137 metres
- Mont Blanc 4810 metres
- Colima Volcano 4330 metres
- Mount Erebus 3795 metres
- Mount Fuji 3776 metres
- Mount Etna 3329 metres
- Mount Olympus 2919 metres
- Mount Pinatubo 1485 metres
- Table Mountain 1086 metres
- Mount Rushmore 1078 metres
- Angel Falls 979 metres

8500 m
8000 m
7500 m
7000 m
6500 m
6000 m
5500 m
5000 m
4500 m
4000 m
3500 m
3000 m
2500 m
2000 m
1500 m
1000 m
500 m
0 m

World map

The countries of the world are divided into seven continents, or areas. The continents are surrounded by *oceans*. The *Equator* is a line on maps that shows the middle of the Earth.

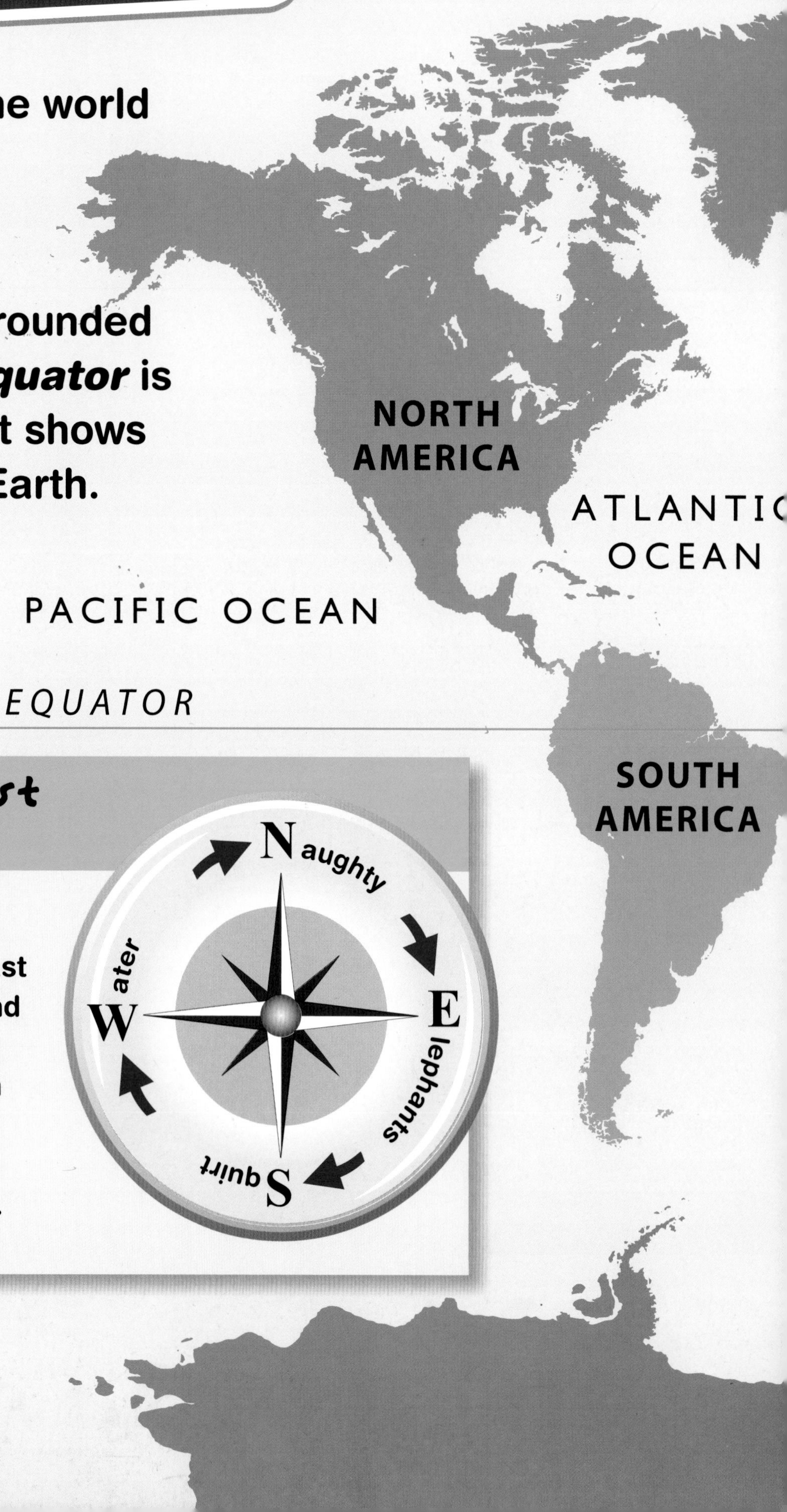

NORTH AMERICA

ATLANTIC OCEAN

PACIFIC OCEAN

EQUATOR

SOUTH AMERICA

North, south, east and west

A *compass* shows what direction north, south, east and west are in. North and south point to the North and South poles. You can say 'Naughty Elephants Squirt Water' to help you remember the directions.

Naughty
Elephants
Squirt
Water

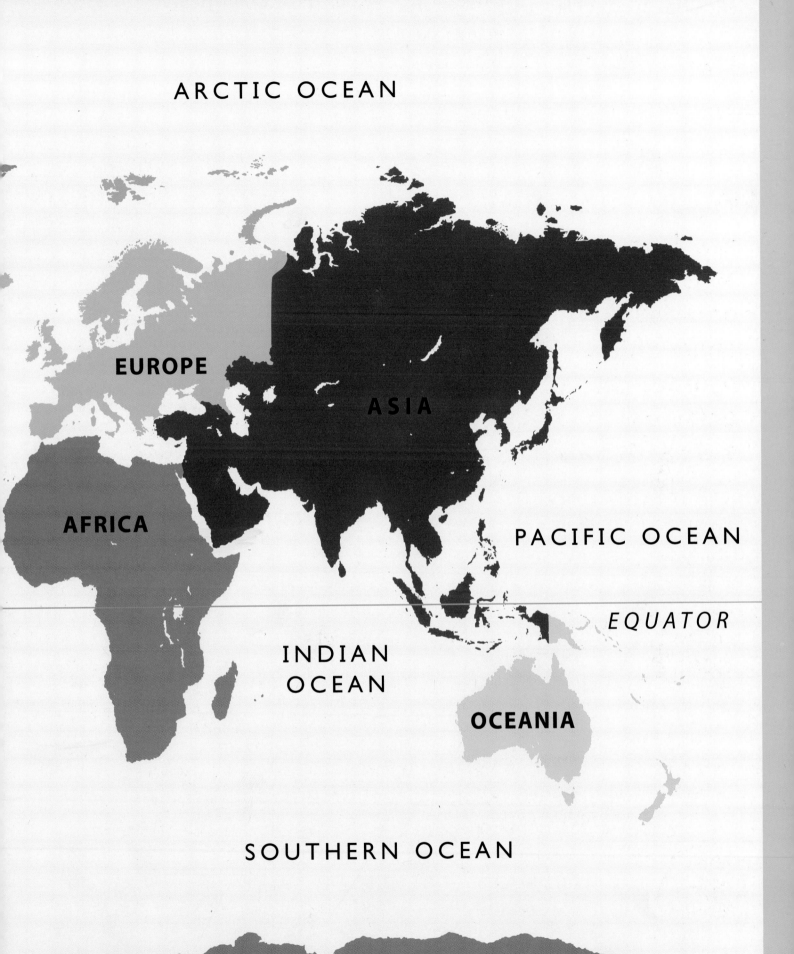

ARCTIC OCEAN

EUROPE

ASIA

AFRICA

PACIFIC OCEAN

EQUATOR

INDIAN
OCEAN

OCEANIA

SOUTHERN OCEAN

ANTARCTICA

Canada

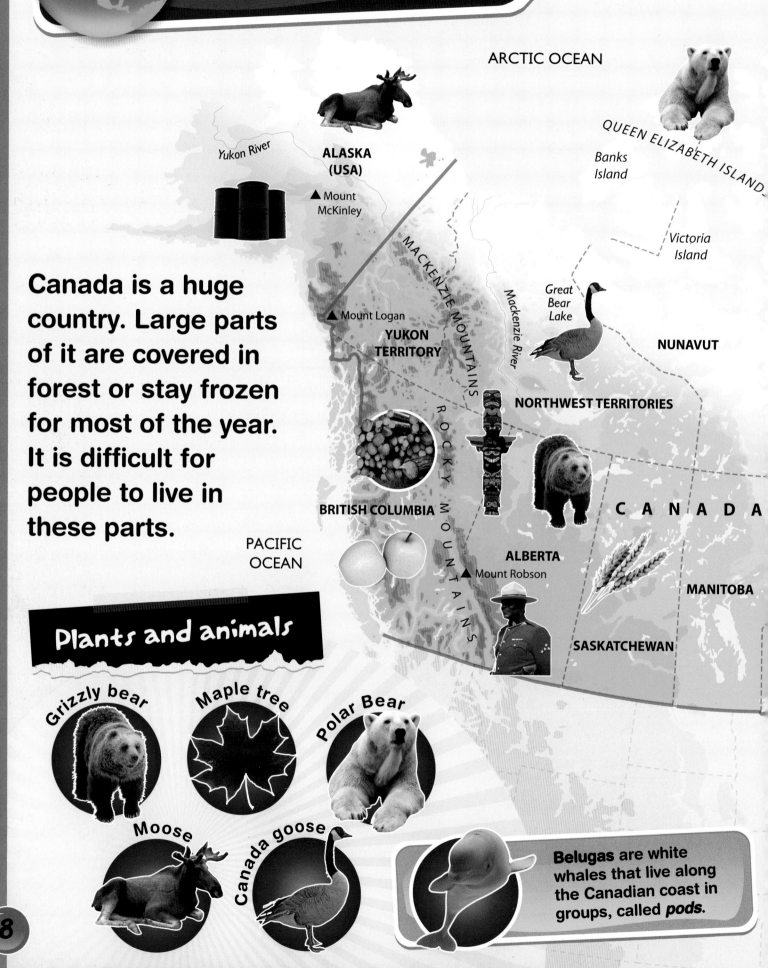

ARCTIC OCEAN

QUEEN ELIZABETH ISLAND

Banks Island

Victoria Island

Yukon River

ALASKA (USA)

▲ Mount McKinley

MACKENZIE MOUNTAINS

Mackenzie River

Great Bear Lake

NUNAVUT

▲ Mount Logan

YUKON TERRITORY

Canada is a huge country. Large parts of it are covered in forest or stay frozen for most of the year. It is difficult for people to live in these parts.

R O C K Y   M O U N T A I N S

NORTHWEST TERRITORIES

BRITISH COLUMBIA

C A N A D A

PACIFIC OCEAN

ALBERTA

▲ Mount Robson

MANITOBA

SASKATCHEWAN

Plants and animals

Grizzly bear

Maple tree

Polar Bear

Moose

Canada goose

Belugas are white whales that live along the Canadian coast in groups, called *pods*.

People and places

Totem pole

Lake Superior

Inuit people

Mountie

Quebec

The **CN Tower** in Ontario is North America's tallest tower. It is 553 metres tall.

Baffin Island

HUDSON BAY

LABRADOR SEA

NEWFOUNDLAND AND LABRADOR

Newfoundland

ONTARIO

QUEBEC

PRINCE EDWARD ISLAND

NEW BRUNSWICK

NOVA SCOTIA

Lake Superior

Ottawa●

Lake Huron

Lake Ontario

Lake Erie

ATLANTIC OCEAN

Produce and resources

Fish

Apples

Timber

Oil

Wheat

Ice hockey is a popular sport in Canada. It is played on *rinks* or frozen lakes.

Western USA

The United States of America, or the USA, is made up of 50 states. The western states have everything from high mountains to sandy deserts and *volcanic* islands.

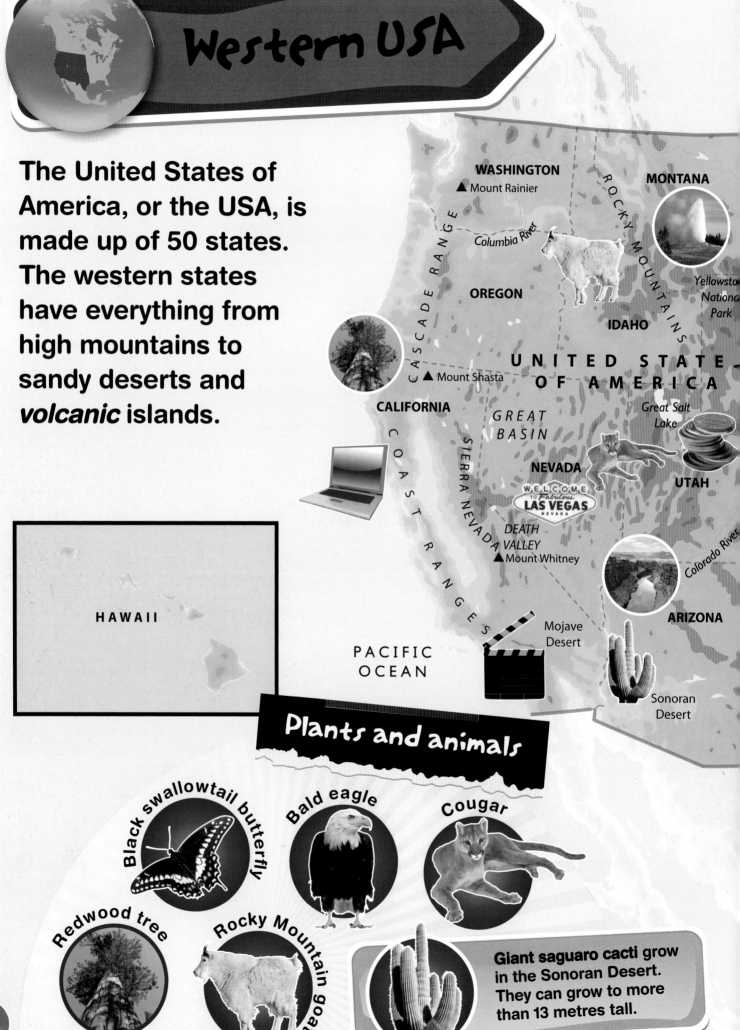

WASHINGTON
▲ Mount Rainier

MONTANA

Columbia River

CASCADE RANGE

OREGON

ROCKY MOUNTAINS

Yellowstone National Park

IDAHO

▲ Mount Shasta

UNITED STATE OF AMERICA

CALIFORNIA

GREAT BASIN

Great Salt Lake

COAST RANGES

SIERRA NEVADA

NEVADA

UTAH

WELCOME TO Fabulous LAS VEGAS NEVADA

DEATH VALLEY
▲ Mount Whitney

Colorado River

ARIZONA

Mojave Desert

PACIFIC OCEAN

Sonoran Desert

HAWAII

Plants and animals

Black swallowtail butterfly

Bald eagle

Cougar

Redwood tree

Rocky Mountain goat

Giant saguaro cacti grow in the Sonoran Desert. They can grow to more than 13 metres tall.

People and places

Old Faithful Geyser

Cowboys

Mount Rushmore

Grand Canyon

Native Americans

Hollywood in California is well known for its *movie studios* and famous actors.

Missouri River

GREAT PLAINS

NORTH DAKOTA

SOUTH DAKOTA

NEBRASKA

WYOMING

Mount Elbert
COLORADO

ROCKY MOUNTAINS

KANSAS

OKLAHOMA

NEW MEXICO

TEXAS

Produce and resources

Computers

Entertainment

WELCOME TO Fabulous LAS VEGAS NEVADA

Skiing

Cattle

Copper

Farms on the Great Plains grow more **wheat** than anywhere else in the world.

11

People and places

Sears Tower

American football

Appalachian Mountains

Cape Canaveral

Statue of Liberty

Eastern USA

Eastern USA stretches from Minnesota to Florida. The capital of the United States, Washington D.C., is in the east.

The White House in Washington D.C. is the home of the President of the USA.

Lake Superior

Lake Michigan

Lake Huron

Lake Erie

Lake Ontario

Washington D.C.

Missouri River

Ohio River

U N I T E D   S T A T E S   O F   A M E R I C A

A P P A L A C H I A N   M O U N T A I N S

MINNESOTA

IOWA

WISCONSIN

ILLINOIS

INDIANA

OHIO

MICHIGAN

MAINE

VERMONT

NEW HAMPSHIRE

MASSACHUSETTS

RHODE ISLAND

CONNECTICUT

NEW YORK

PENNSYLVANIA

NEW JERSEY

MARYLAND

DELAWARE

WEST VIRGINIA

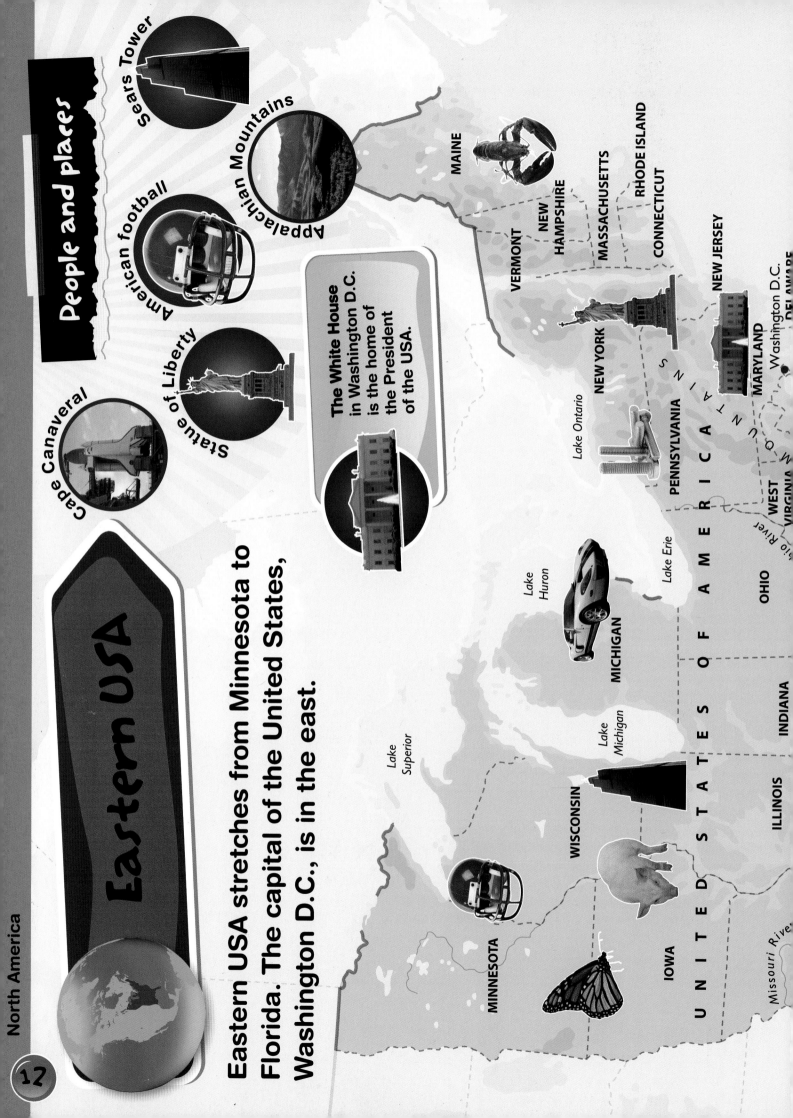

Produce and resources

Oranges

Jazz

Cars

Steel

Pigs

The USA is one of the biggest cotton growers in the world.

ATLANTIC OCEAN

VIRGINIA

NORTH CAROLINA

▲ Mount Mitchell

APPALACHIA

SOUTH CAROLINA

KENTUCKY

TENNESSEE

GEORGIA

ALABAMA

MISSOURI

ARKANSAS

MISSISSIPPI

Mississippi River

LOUISIANA

GULF OF MEXICO

FLORIDA

Plants and animals

Florida manatee

Prairie dog

Alligator

Lobster

Palmetto tree

Each year, millions of monarch butterflies fly from northern USA to Mexico.

Mexico and Central America

Sonoran Desert

GULF OF CALIFORNIA

BAJA CALIFORNIA

SIERRA MADRE OCCIDENTAL

Rio Grande

SIERRA MADRE ORIENTAL

MEXICO

GULF OF MEXICO

Lake Chapala

● Mexico City

▲ Pico de Orizaba

YUCATÁN PENINSULA

PACIFIC OCEAN

BELIZE
Belmopan

GUATEMALA
Guatemala City ●

HONDUR
Tegucigal

San Salvador ●
EL SALVADOR

Managua

Central America is a strip of land linking the continents of North and South America. Mexico lies to the north of Central America, while the Caribbean Islands lie to the east.

Plants and animals

Prickly pear cactus

Toucan

Cuban Trogon

Scarlet ibis

Rainforest

Howler monkeys live in the Yucatán Peninsula in Mexico.

Panama Canal

Tikal Ruins

Colima Volcano

Kuna people

Rio Grande River

ATLANTIC OCEAN

Mexico City is the capital of Mexico. It is one of the biggest cities in the world.

BAHAMAS

● Nassau

TURKS AND CAICOS ISLANDS

● Havana

CUBA

CAYMAN ISLANDS

HAITI
Port-au-Prince ●

DOMINICAN REPUBLIC
● Santo Domingo

VIRGIN ISLANDS ANGUILLA ST. MARTIN
ST. BARTHÉLEMY
SABA **ANTIGUA AND BARBUDA**
PUERTO RICO ST. EUSTATIUS Basseterre ● St. John's
ST. KITTS AND NEVIS
GUADELOUPE
DOMINICA
Roseau ●
MONTSERRAT MARTINIQUE
Castries ● **BARBADOS**
ST. LUCIA
Kingstown ● Bridgetown
ST. VINCENT AND
GRENADA **THE GRENADINES**
St George's ●

JAMAICA ●
Kingston

C A R I B B E A N   S E A

CURAÇAO
ARUBA
BONAIRE

TRINIDAD AND TOBAGO
Port-of-Spain ●

NICARAGUA

COSTA RICA
San José

● Panama City

PANAMA

Sugar cane

Silver

Bananas

Textiles, or fabrics, made in Central America can be very brightly coloured.

Coffee

Cricket

North America

15

People and places

Amazon River

Itaipu Dam

Brasilia Cathedral

Kayapo people

Carnival

Angel Falls in Venezuela is the world's highest waterfall. It is 979 metres from top to bottom.

ATLANTIC OCEAN

Brazil and its neighbours

Brazil is the largest country in South America. It also has the biggest *population*. Many different languages are spoken in South America, such as Spanish, Portuguese, English and Dutch.

Caracas
VENEZUELA
Angel Falls
GUIANA HIGHLANDS
Lake Maracaibo
Orinoco River
Georgetown
GUYANA
Paramaribo
SURINAME
FRENCH GUIANA
Negro River
Amazon River
AMAZON BASIN

Produce and resources

Cotton

Soya beans

Timber

Football

Wool

Brazil nuts, fruit and rubber come from the Amazon rainforest.

Plants and animals

Jaguar

Scarlet Macaw

Piranha

Rubber tree

Giant water lily

Rare golden lion tamarin monkeys live in an area of forest on Brazil's east coast.

BRAZIL

MATO GROSSO

BRAZILIAN HIGHLANDS

● Brasilia

▲ Sugar Loaf Mountain

Paraná River

PARAGUAY

● Asunción

URUGUAY

● Montevideo

Along the Andes

The Andes Mountains stretch the length of South America. They run from Colombia in the north to Chile in the south.

People and places

Gauchos

Machu Picchu

Moreno Glacier

Cotopaxi Volcano

Lake Titicaca

The Atacama Desert in Chile is the driest place on Earth. In some parts, no rain has fallen for years.

Pico Cristóbal Colón ▲

● Bogotá
COLOMBIA

● Quito
ECUADOR

PERU

▲ Huascarán

● Lima

Amazon River

ANDES MOUNTAIN

Lake Titicaca

BOLIVIA

GALÁPAGOS ISLANDS

Produce and resources

ATLANTIC OCEAN

Emeralds

Coffee

Copper

Sheep

Sardines

Grapes are grown in *vineyards* in Chile. Most of them are used to make wine.

PACIFIC OCEAN

Paraná River

ANDES MOUNTAINS

Atacama Desert

CHILE

Valparaíso ● Santiago ●
▲ Cerro Aconcagua

ARGENTINA

Buenos Aires

PATAGONIA

FALKLAND ISLANDS

Tierra del Fuego

Cape Horn

Plants and animals

Mangrove swamp

Andean tapir

Andean condor

Magellan penguin

Spectacled bear

People living in the Andes keep llamas for carrying goods and for meat, milk and wool.

North Africa and the Sahara

Parts of north Africa are covered by the Sahara Desert, the largest desert in the world. Many *coastal* areas have less dry weather, so *crops* can grow well.

ATLANTIC OCEAN

Strait of Gibraltar

CEUTA   MELILLA

●Algiers   ●Tunis

MADEIRA

Rabat●

MOROCCO   ATLAS MOUNTAINS   **TUNISIA**   MEDITERRANEAN SEA

Mount Toubkal▲   Tripoli●

CANARY ISLANDS   **ALGERIA**   ●Surt

S a h a r a   D e s e r t

WESTERN SAHARA   **LIBYA**

A H A G G A R MOUNTAINS   Libyan De...

MAURITANIA

Nouakchott●

Plants and animals

Tamarind tree

Nile crocodile

Camel

Gelada

Scorpion

The **fennec fox's** large ears keep it cool by letting heat escape from its body.

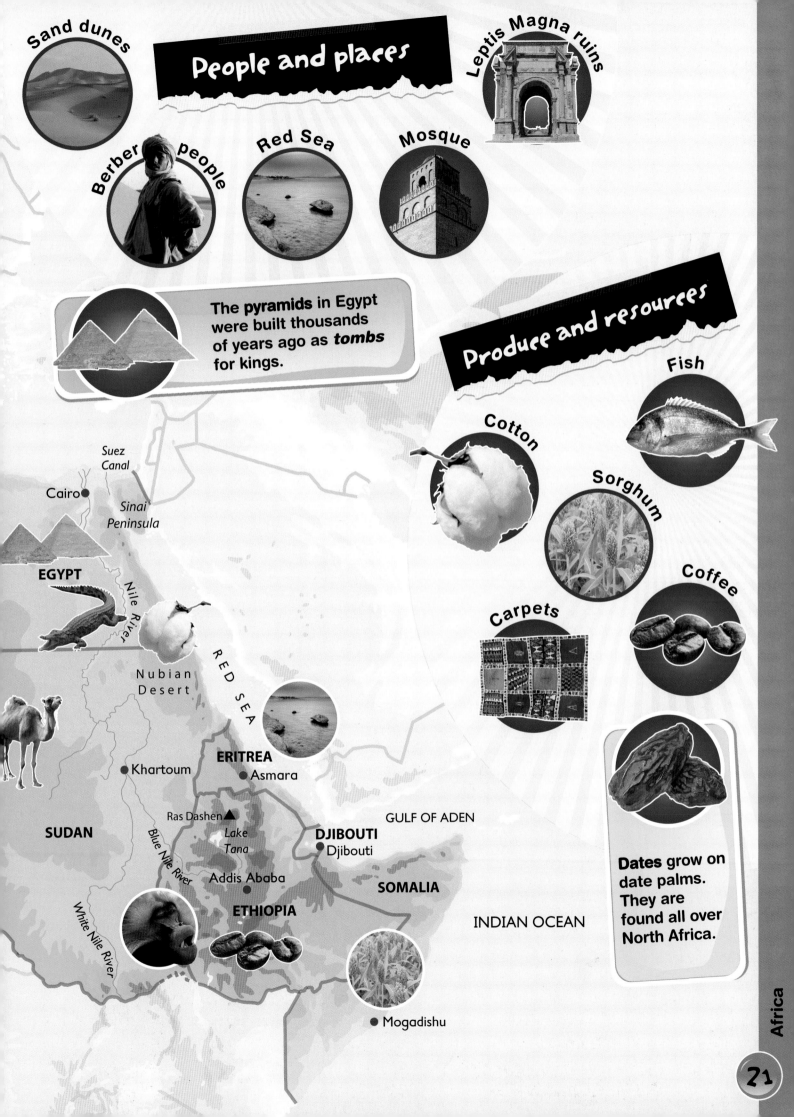

Sand dunes

People and places

Leptis Magna ruins

Berber people

Red Sea

Mosque

The **pyramids** in Egypt were built thousands of years ago as *tombs* for kings.

Produce and resources

Fish

Cotton

Sorghum

Coffee

Carpets

Suez Canal

Cairo

Sinai Peninsula

EGYPT

Nile River

Nubian Desert

RED SEA

Khartoum

ERITREA

Asmara

Ras Dashen ▲

Blue Nile River

Lake Tana

GULF OF ADEN

DJIBOUTI

Djibouti

SUDAN

Addis Ababa

SOMALIA

ETHIOPIA

White Nile River

INDIAN OCEAN

Dates grow on date palms. They are found all over North Africa.

Mogadishu

West, Central and East Africa

West, Central and East Africa stretches from Senegal in the west to Kenya in the east. In the west and centre are *rainforests*. In the north and east are *grasslands*.

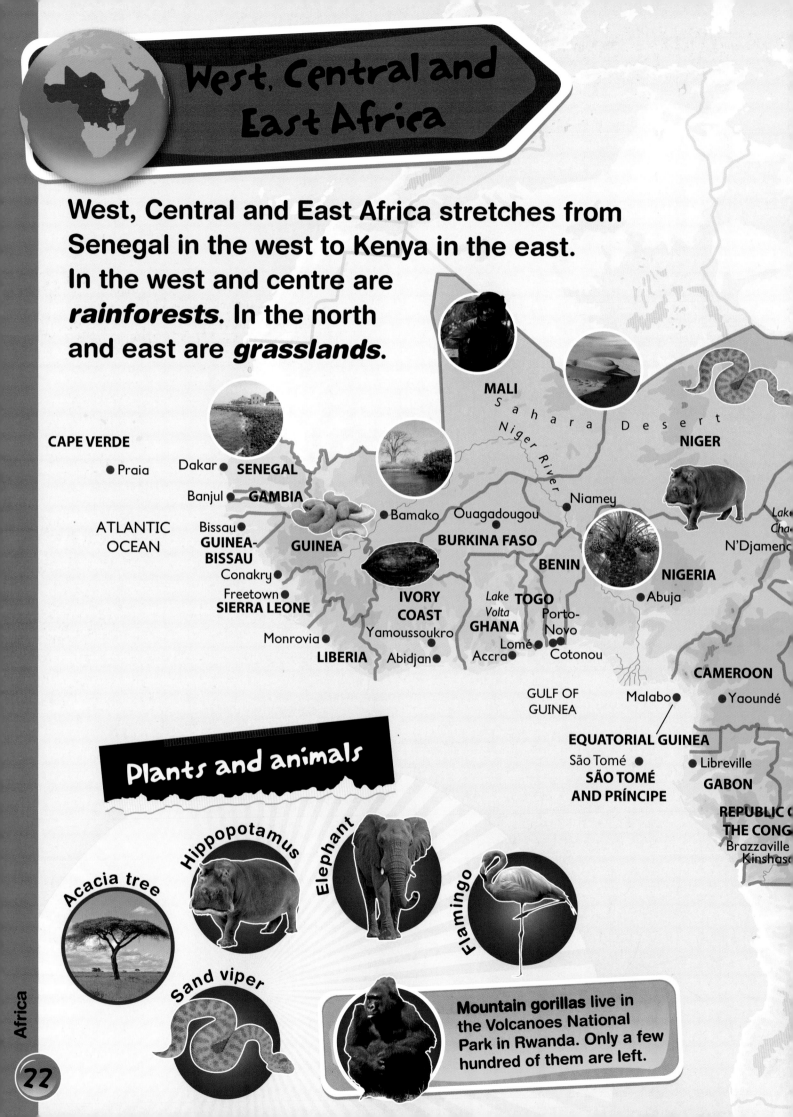

MALI
S a h a r a   D e s e r t
Niger River

NIGER

CAPE VERDE

• Praia   Dakar • **SENEGAL**

Banjul • **GAMBIA**

Niamey •

ATLANTIC
OCEAN

Bissau •
**GUINEA-
BISSAU**   **GUINEA**

Bamako •   Ouagadougou •
BURKINA FASO

Lake
Cha

N'Djamena

Conakry •

Freetown •
SIERRA LEONE

BENIN

NIGERIA

• Abuja

**IVORY
COAST**

Lake
Volta   **TOGO**
Porto-
Novo

GHANA

Yamoussoukro •

Lomé •

Monrovia •

LIBERIA   • Abidjan

Accra •   Cotonou •

CAMEROON

GULF OF
GUINEA

Malabo •   • Yaoundé

EQUATORIAL GUINEA

São Tomé •   • Libreville
**SÃO TOMÉ
AND PRÍNCIPE**   **GABON**

**REPUBLIC O
THE CONG**
Brazzaville
Kinshasa

Plants and animals

Acacia tree

Hippopotamus

Elephant

Flamingo

Sand viper

Mountain gorillas live in the Volcanoes National Park in Rwanda. Only a few hundred of them are left.

People and places

Tuareg people

Maasai people

Niger River

Sahara Desert

Dakar

Mount Kilimanjaro is the tallest mountain in Africa. It is more than 5890 metres high.

CHAD

CENTRAL AFRICAN REPUBLIC

Bangui

Congo River

DEMOCRATIC REPUBLIC OF THE CONGO

UGANDA

Kampala ●

Lake Turkana

Lake Victoria

RWANDA ● Kigali

Bujumbura ●
BURUNDI

Lake Tanganyika

GREAT RIFT VALLEY

KENYA

▲ Mount Kenya

● Nairobi

▲ Mount Kilimanjaro

Dodoma ●

● Dar es Salaam

TANZANIA

Produce and resources

Palm oil

Diamonds

Cocoa

Cashew nuts

Cattle

Cassava root is one of the most widely eaten foods in Africa.

Southern Africa

Hot, dry deserts stretch across large areas of southern Africa. The island of Madagascar lies to the east. Lots of amazing **wildlife** lives there.

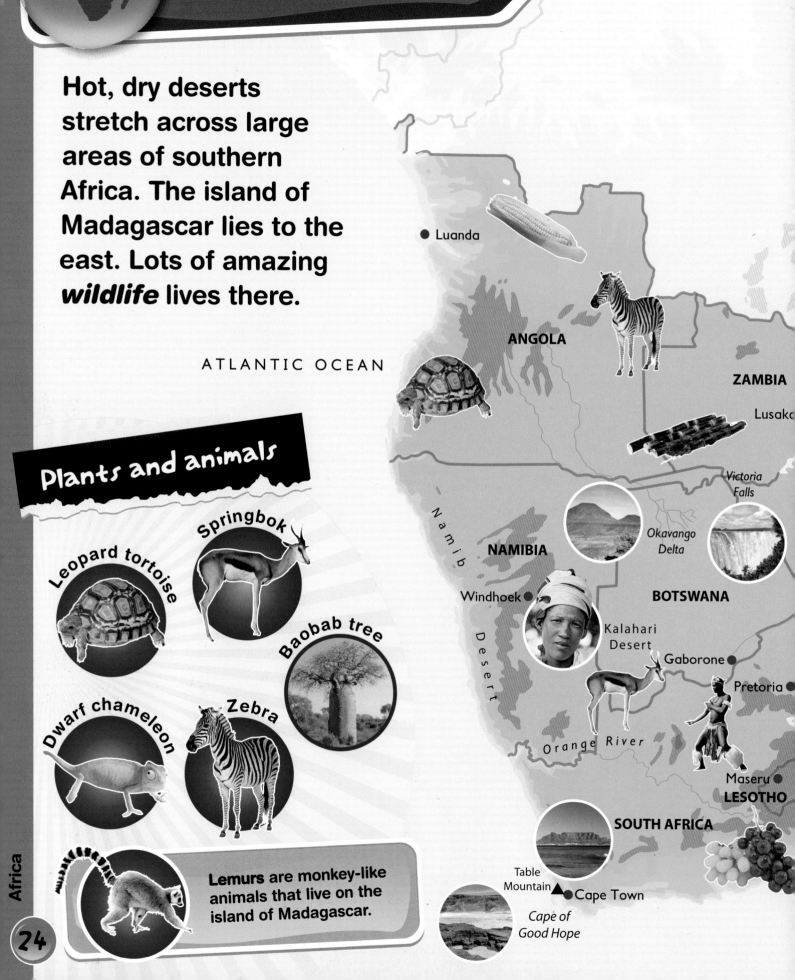

ATLANTIC OCEAN

Plants and animals

Leopard tortoise

Springbok

Baobab tree

Dwarf chameleon

Zebra

Lemurs are monkey-like animals that live on the island of Madagascar.

Luanda

ANGOLA

ZAMBIA

Lusaka

Victoria Falls

Okavango Delta

Namib Desert

NAMIBIA

Windhoek

BOTSWANA

Kalahari Desert

Gaborone

Pretoria

Orange River

Maseru

LESOTHO

SOUTH AFRICA

Table Mountain

Cape Town

Cape of Good Hope

People and places

Victoria Falls

Zulu people

Cape of Good Hope

San people

Kalahari Desert

Table Mountain has a very flat top. It is just outside Cape Town in South Africa.

● Victoria

SEYCHELLES

● Moroni

INDIAN OCEAN

COMOROS MAYOTTE

Lake Malawi

●Lilongwe

MALAWI

Zambezi River

● Harare

MBABWE

MOZAMBIQUE CHANNEL

MADAGASCAR

● Antananarivo

MAURITIUS

● Port Louis

REUNION

MOZAMBIQUE

Limpopo River

● Maputo
Mbabane
Lobamba
WAZILAND

Produce and resources

Shellfish

Grapes

Cloves

Maize

Sugar cane

Tourism is a large industry in southern Africa. People travel here to go on *safari*.

Northern Europe stretches from the Republic of Ireland in the west to Latvia in the east. Northern parts such as Norway and Sweden can be very cold. Thick forests grow in some of these countries.

Plants and animals

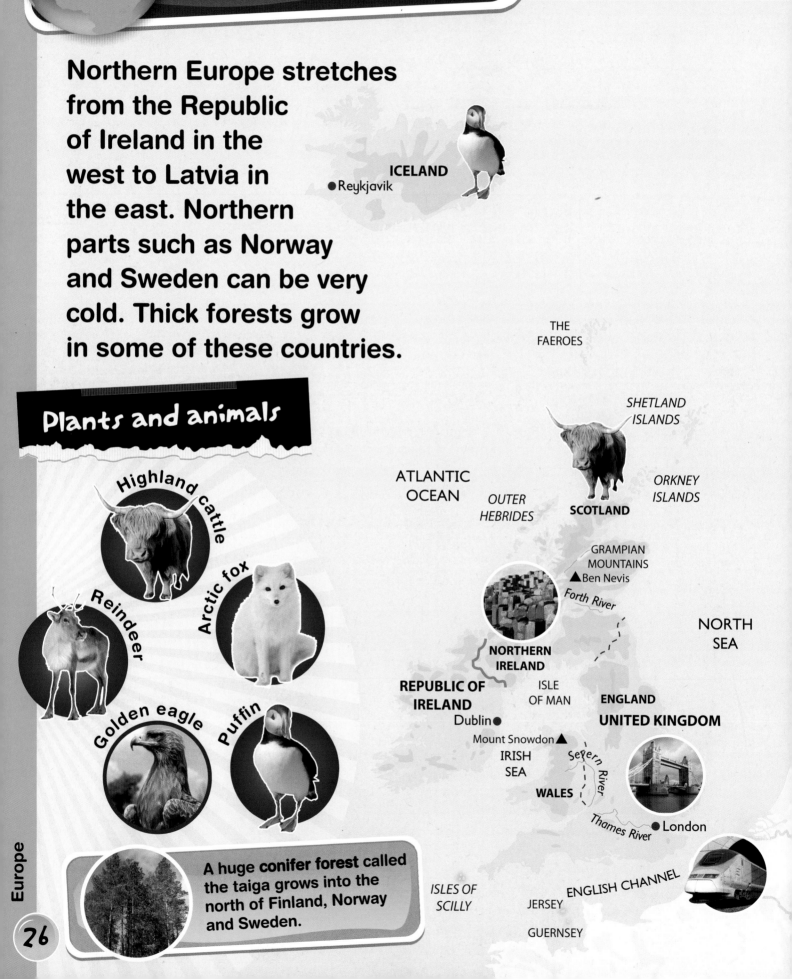

Highland cattle

Reindeer

Arctic fox

Golden eagle

Puffin

ICELAND
●Reykjavik

THE FAEROES

SHETLAND ISLANDS

ATLANTIC OCEAN

OUTER HEBRIDES

ORKNEY ISLANDS

SCOTLAND

GRAMPIAN MOUNTAINS
▲Ben Nevis

Forth River

NORTH SEA

NORTHERN IRELAND

REPUBLIC OF IRELAND

ISLE OF MAN

ENGLAND

Dublin●

UNITED KINGDOM

Mount Snowdon ▲

IRISH SEA

Severn River

WALES

Thames River ●London

ISLES OF SCILLY

JERSEY

ENGLISH CHANNEL

GUERNSEY

A huge conifer forest called the taiga grows into the north of Finland, Norway and Sweden.

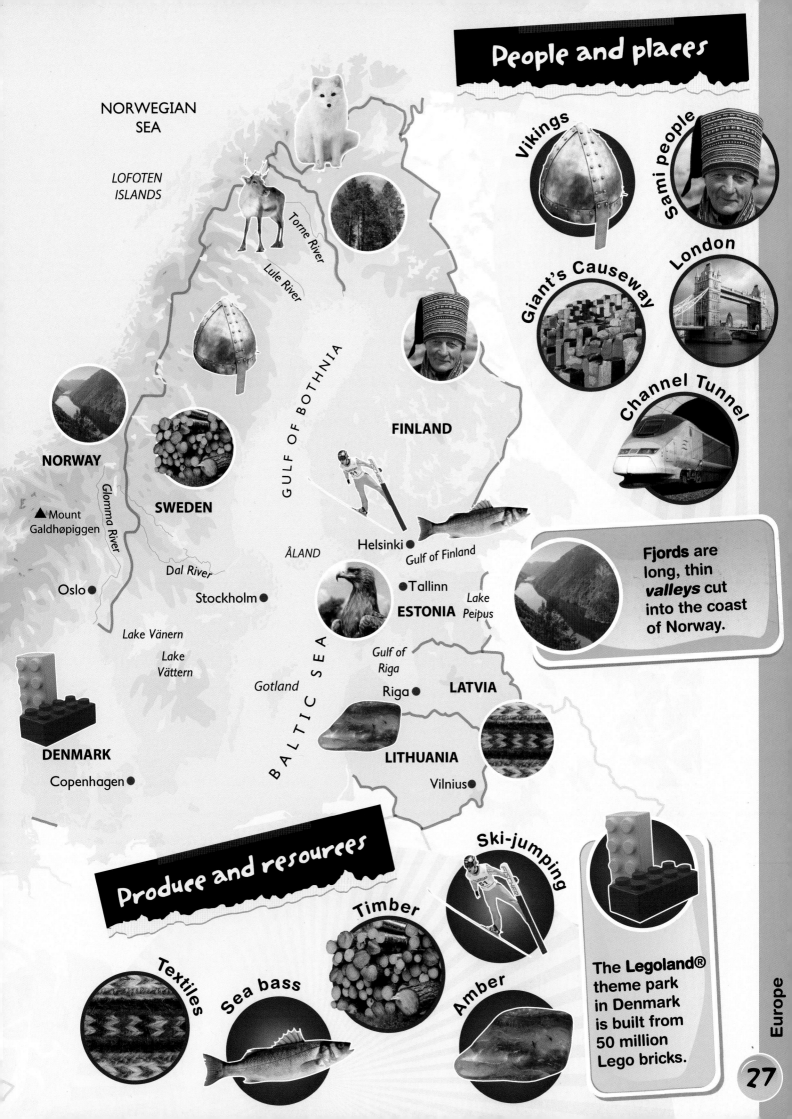

NORWEGIAN SEA

LOFOTEN ISLANDS

Vikings

Sami people

Giant's Causeway

London

Channel Tunnel

Torne River

Lule River

GULF OF BOTHNIA

FINLAND

NORWAY

Glomma River

▲ Mount Galdhøpiggen

SWEDEN

Dal River

ÅLAND

Helsinki ●

Gulf of Finland

Oslo ●

Stockholm ●

Lake Vänern

Lake Vättern

Tallinn ●

ESTONIA

Lake Peipus

Gotland

BALTIC SEA

Gulf of Riga

Riga ●

LATVIA

LITHUANIA

Vilnius ●

DENMARK

Copenhagen ●

Fjords are long, thin **valleys** cut into the coast of Norway.

Ski-jumping

Timber

Textiles

Sea bass

Amber

The **Legoland®** theme park in Denmark is built from 50 million Lego bricks.

Western Europe

Western Europe has many mountain ranges, lakes and forests. The coastal areas of the Mediterranean Sea can be very hot in summer. Many *tourists* visit this *region* every year.

ENGLISH CHANNEL

Paris

Loire River

FRANCE

BAY OF BISCAY

ATLANTIC OCEAN

MASSIF CENTRAL

PYRENEES MOUNTAINS

Ebro River

ANDORRA
Andorra la Vella

IBERIAN MOUNTAINS

SPAIN

Madrid

PORTUGAL

Tagus River

BALEARIC ISLANDS

Lisbon

Guadalquivir River

GIBRALTAR
CEUTA

MELILLA

Plants and animals

Hoopoe

Red deer

Mountain goat

Wild horse

Pine tree

Alpine marmots spend the winter fast asleep in *burrows*, or dens, underneath the ground.

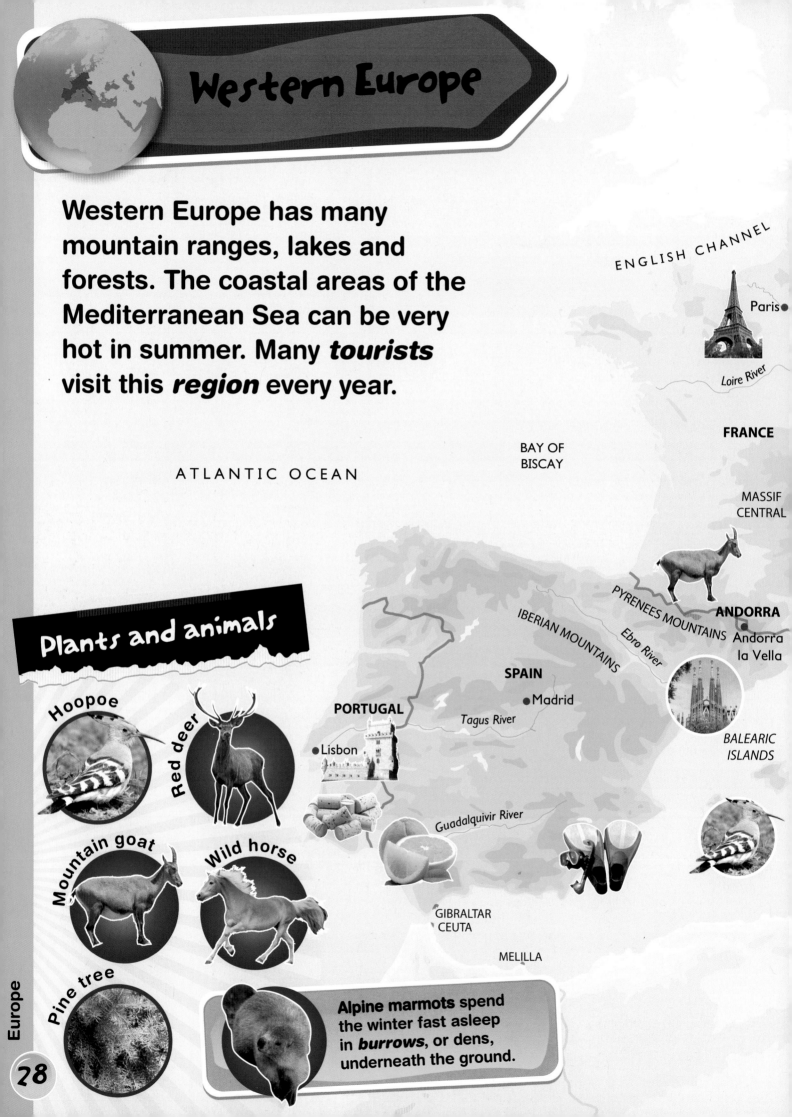

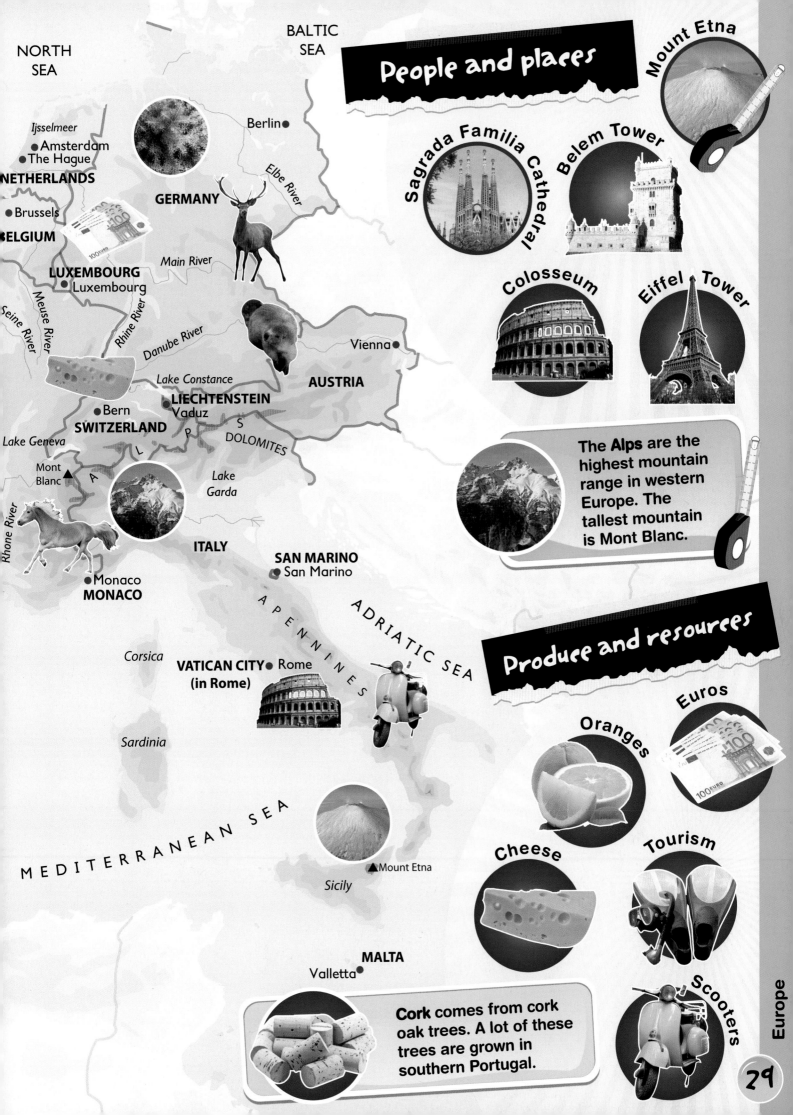

NORTH SEA

BALTIC SEA

People and places

Mount Etna

Ijsselmeer

●Amsterdam
●The Hague

NETHERLANDS

Berlin ●

GERMANY

Elbe River

Sagrada Familia Cathedral

Belem Tower

● Brussels

BELGIUM

Main River

LUXEMBOURG
Luxembourg

Seine River

Meuse River

Rhine River

Danube River

Colosseum

Eiffel Tower

Vienna ●

Lake Constance

LIECHTENSTEIN
Vaduz

AUSTRIA

● Bern

SWITZERLAND

P   S
DOLOMITES

Lake Geneva

Mont Blanc ▲

A   L

Lake Garda

The **Alps** are the highest mountain range in western Europe. The tallest mountain is Mont Blanc.

Rhone River

ITALY

SAN MARINO
San Marino

MONACO
● Monaco

Produce and resources

Corsica

VATICAN CITY
(in Rome)

Rome ●

A P E N N I N E S

A D R I A T I C   S E A

Sardinia

Euros

Oranges

M E D I T E R R A N E A N   S E A

▲ Mount Etna

Sicily

Cheese

Tourism

MALTA
Valletta ●

Scooters

Cork comes from cork oak trees. A lot of these trees are grown in southern Portugal.

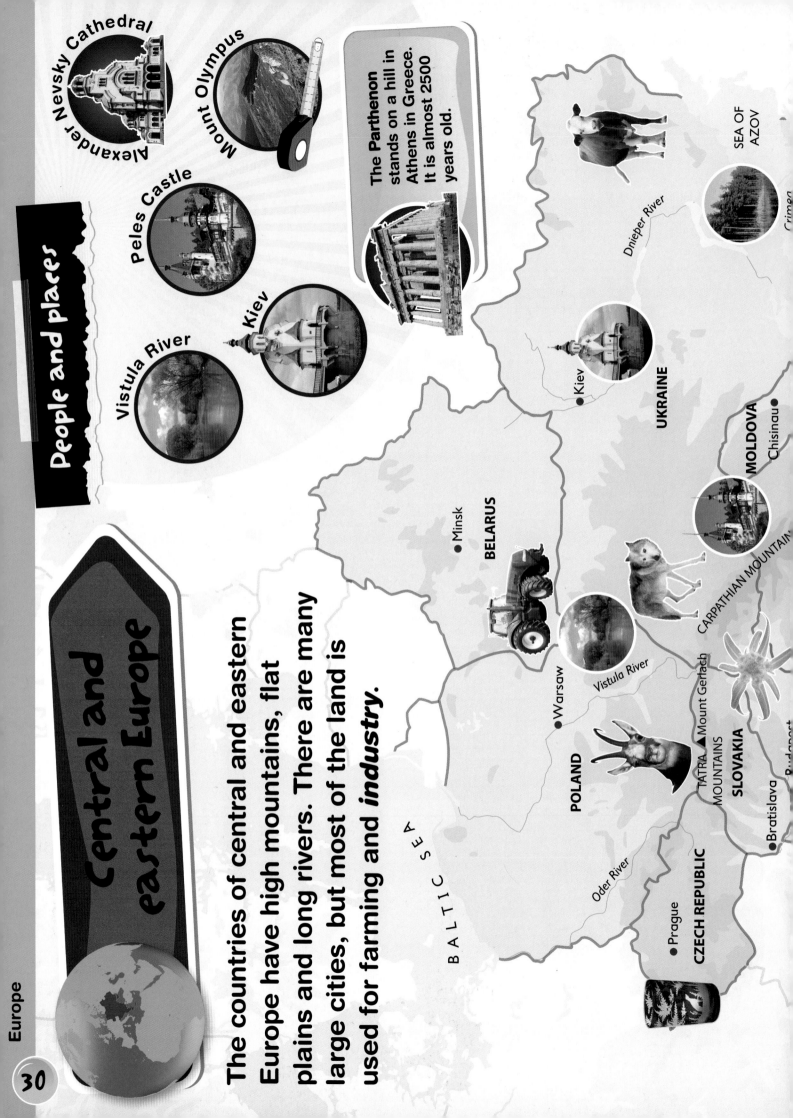

People and places

Alexander Nevsky Cathedral

Mount Olympus

Peles Castle

Vistula River

Kiev

The Parthenon stands on a hill in Athens in Greece. It is almost 2500 years old.

Central and eastern Europe

The countries of central and eastern Europe have high mountains, flat plains and long rivers. There are many large cities, but most of the land is used for farming and *industry*.

BALTIC SEA

Minsk

BELARUS

Warsaw

POLAND

Prague

CZECH REPUBLIC

Oder River

Vistula River

TATRA ▲ Mount Gerlach
MOUNTAINS

SLOVAKIA

Bratislava

Budapest

CARPATHIAN MOUNTAINS

Kiev

UKRAINE

MOLDOVA

Chisinau

Dnieper River

SEA OF AZOV

Crimea

BLACK SEA

Produce and resources

Olive oil

Glass

Cattle

Machinery

Tourism

The roses that grow in Bulgaria are a special type that can be used to make *a scented oil.*

Bucharest
Danube River
Belgrade
Zagreb
Ljubljana

SLOVENIA
HUNGARY
CROATIA
BOSNIA AND HERZEGOVINA
Sarajevo
SERBIA
MONTENEGRO
Podgorica
KOSOVO
Pristina
Skopje
MACEDONIA
Tirane
ALBANIA

BALKAN MOUNTAINS
Sofia
BULGARIA

Mount Olympus
GREECE
Athens

PINDUS MOUNTAINS

AEGEAN SEA

SEA OF CRETE

Crete

MEDITERRANEAN SEA

ADRIATIC SEA

Plants and animals

Grey wolf

Conifer trees

Chamois

Edelweiss

Pelican

Dolphins can be seen swimming next to boats in the Aegean Sea.

Russia and central Asia

Russia is the biggest country in the world. It stretches across the two continents of Europe and Asia. The eight countries of central Asia lie to the southwest of Russia.

BARENTS SEA

RUSSIA

Moscow

URAL MOUNTAINS

R   U   S

Ob River

E

Volga River

BLACK SEA

Mount Elbrus▲

S   T   E   P   P   E

Astana

GEORGIA

CASPIAN SEA

Aral Sea

KAZAKHSTAN

Tbilisi

ARMENIA
Yerevan

AZERBAIJAN
Baku

Lake Balkhash

Amu Darya River

UZBEKISTAN

TURKMENISTAN

Bishkek

Ashgabat

Tashkent

KYRGYZSTAN

Dushanbe

TAJIKISTAN

Plants and animals

Harp seal

Brown bear

Taiga forest

Elk

Wild mushroom

The **Siberian tiger** only lives in the far east of Russia, on the border with China.

Europe

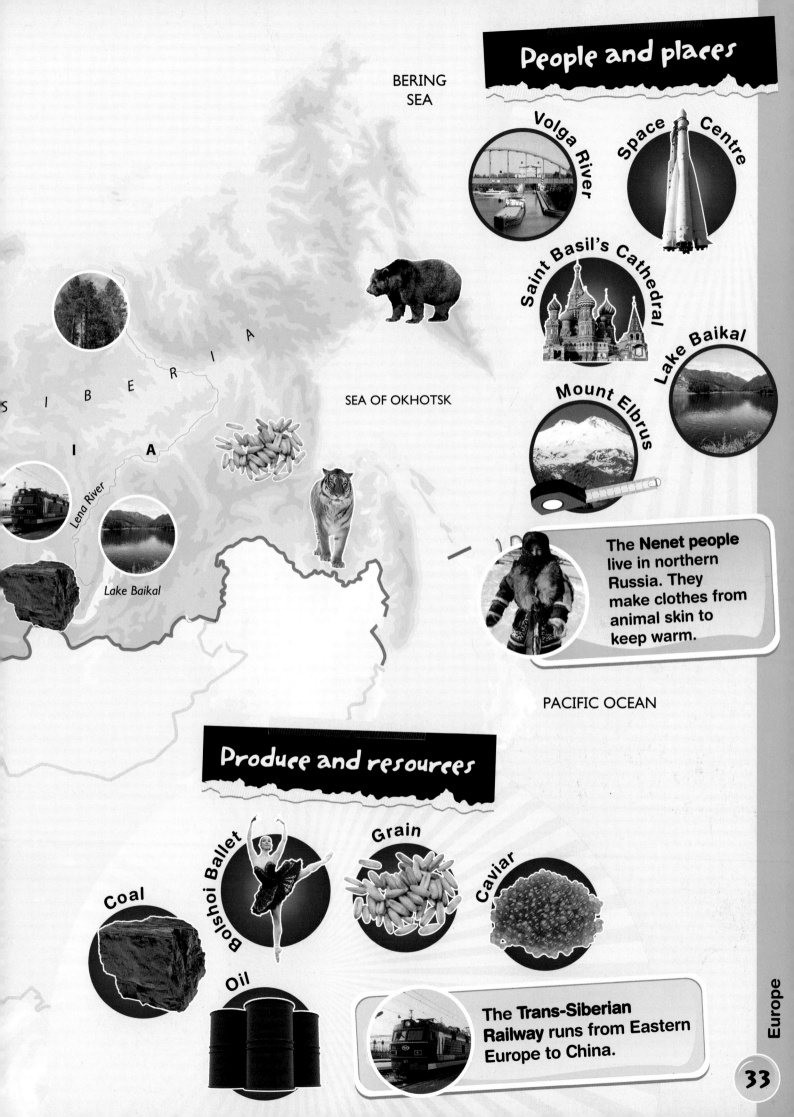

BERING SEA

Volga River

Space Centre

Saint Basil's Cathedral

Lake Baikal

Mount Elbrus

SIBERIA

SEA OF OKHOTSK

Lena River

Lake Baikal

The **Nenet people** live in northern Russia. They make clothes from animal skin to keep warm.

PACIFIC OCEAN

Produce and resources

Coal

Bolshoi Ballet

Grain

Caviar

Oil

The **Trans-Siberian Railway** runs from Eastern Europe to China.

Europe

33

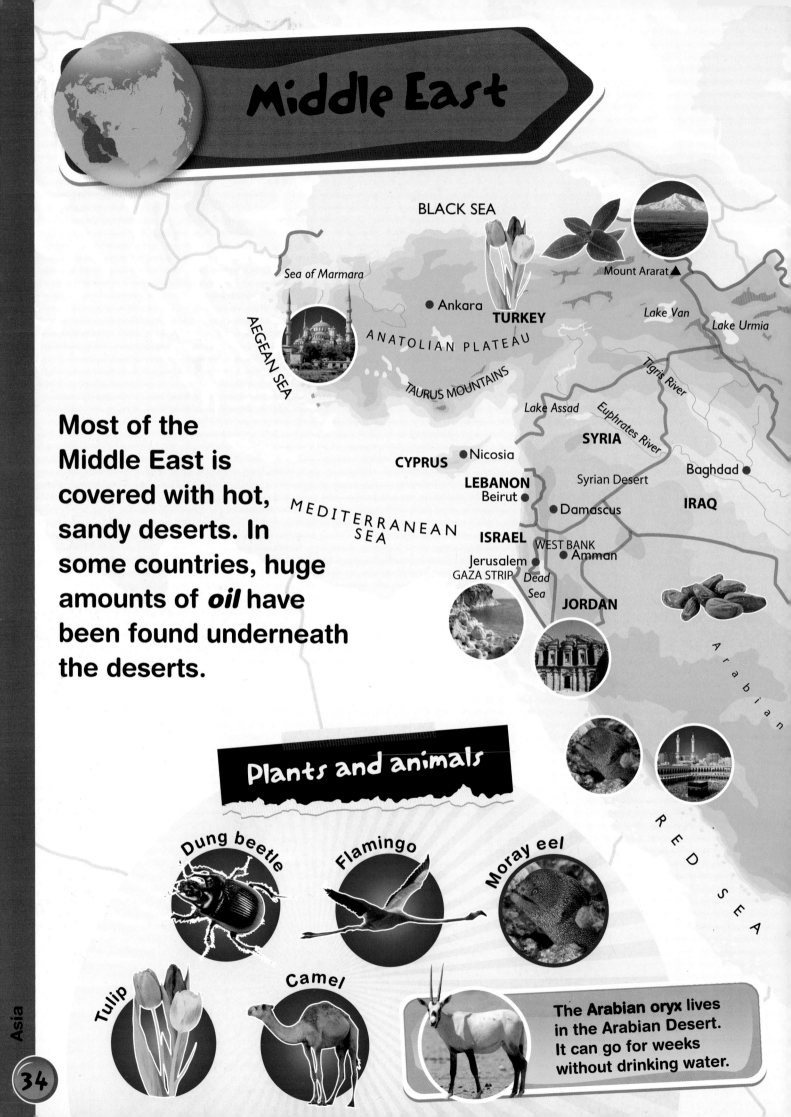

Middle East

BLACK SEA

Sea of Marmara

Ankara
TURKEY

Mount Ararat ▲

Lake Van

Lake Urmia

AEGEAN SEA

A N A T O L I A N   P L A T E A U

TAURUS MOUNTAINS

Tigris River

Lake Assad

Euphrates River

SYRIA

CYPRUS Nicosia

Syrian Desert

Baghdad

MEDITERRANEAN SEA

LEBANON
Beirut

Damascus

IRAQ

ISRAEL
WEST BANK

Jerusalem
GAZA STRIP
Dead Sea

Amman

JORDAN

A r a b i a n

R E D   S E A

Most of the Middle East is covered with hot, sandy deserts. In some countries, huge amounts of *oil* have been found underneath the deserts.

Plants and animals

Dung beetle

Flamingo

Moray eel

Tulip

Camel

The **Arabian oryx** lives in the Arabian Desert. It can go for weeks without drinking water.

Burj-Al-Arab Hotel

Petra ruins

Mount Ararat

Kaaba building

Blue Mosque

The **Dead Sea** is a lake between Israel and Jordan. It is so salty, you can float in the water.

CASPIAN SEA

▲ Mount Demavend
● Tehran

Kavir Desert

IRAN

Lut Desert

ZAGROS MOUNTAINS

KUWAIT
● Kuwait City

GULF OF OMAN

BAHRAIN
Manama ● **QATAR**
● Doha

● Muscat

● Abu Dhabi

UNITED ARAB EMIRATES

OMAN

ARABIAN SEA

● Riyadh

SAUDI ARABIA

Desert

Rub 'al Khali (Empty Quarter)

YEMEN

● Sanaa

Sheep

Wheat

Dates

Coffee

Tea

Iran is famous for its handmade Persian **carpets**. They are made of wool.

People and places

Southern Asia

Sri Meenakshi Temple

Drupka people

Thar Desert

Mount Everest

Ganges River

The Taj Mahal in India was built as a tomb for an Indian *empress* more than 400 years ago.

AFGHANISTAN
Kabul •

PAKISTAN
Islamabad •
Indus River
Thar Desert

Delhi •

H I M A L A Y A S
Mount Everest ▲

NEPAL
Kathmandu •

BHUTAN
Thimphu •

BANGLADESH
Dhaka •
Brahmaputra River

Ganges River

Narmada River

INDIA

BAY OF BENGAL

India is the largest country in southern Asia. Mount Everest, the highest mountain in the world, is in the Himalayas, to the north east of India.

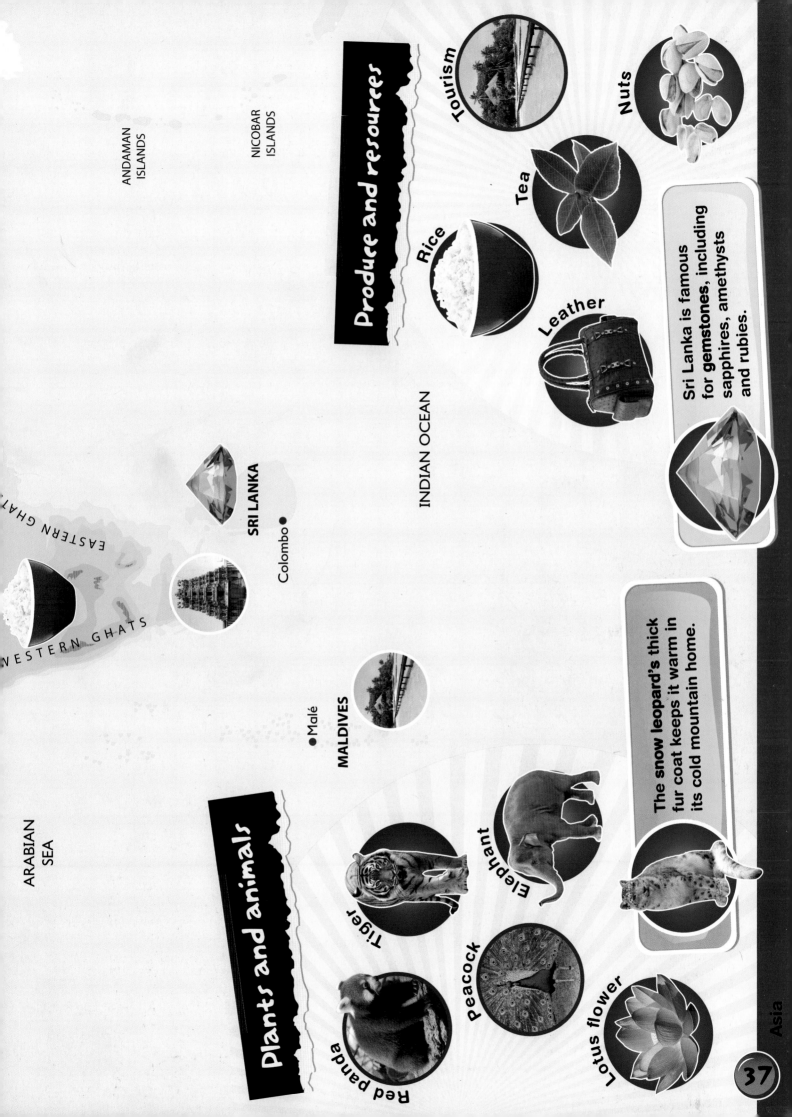

ANDAMAN
ISLANDS

NICOBAR
ISLANDS

Produce and resources

Tourism

Nuts

Tea

Rice

Leather

Sri Lanka is famous for gemstones, including sapphires, amethysts and rubies.

INDIAN OCEAN

EASTERN GHATS

WESTERN GHATS

SRI LANKA

Colombo ●

Malé ●

MALDIVES

The snow leopard's thick fur coat keeps it warm in its cold mountain home.

ARABIAN
SEA

Plants and animals

Tiger

Elephant

Peacock

Red panda

Lotus flower

South East Asia

South East Asia is a hot, rainy area, made up of a small piece of **mainland** and many small islands. The country of Indonesia alone has more than 3000 islands.

Hkakabo Razi

Irrawaddy River

Salween River

BURMA

Naypyidaw

VIETNAM
Hanoi

LAOS

Vientiane

THAILAND

Bangkok

ANDAMAN SEA

Mekong River

SOUTH CHINA SEA

CAMBODIA

Phnom Penh

MALAYSIA

Putrajaya
Kuala Lumpur
SINGAPORE
Singapore

BARISAN MOUNTAINS

Sumatra

INDIAN OCEAN

JAVA SEA

Anak Krakatoa ▲
Jakarta
Java

Plants and animals

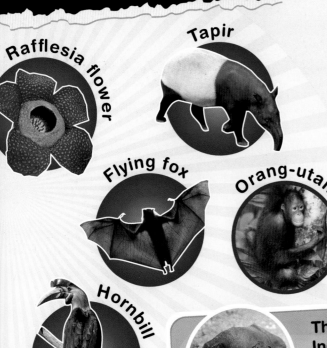

Rafflesia flower

Tapir

Flying fox

Orang-utan

Hornbill

The **Komodo dragon** of Indonesia grows up to 3 metres long and is the world's largest lizard.

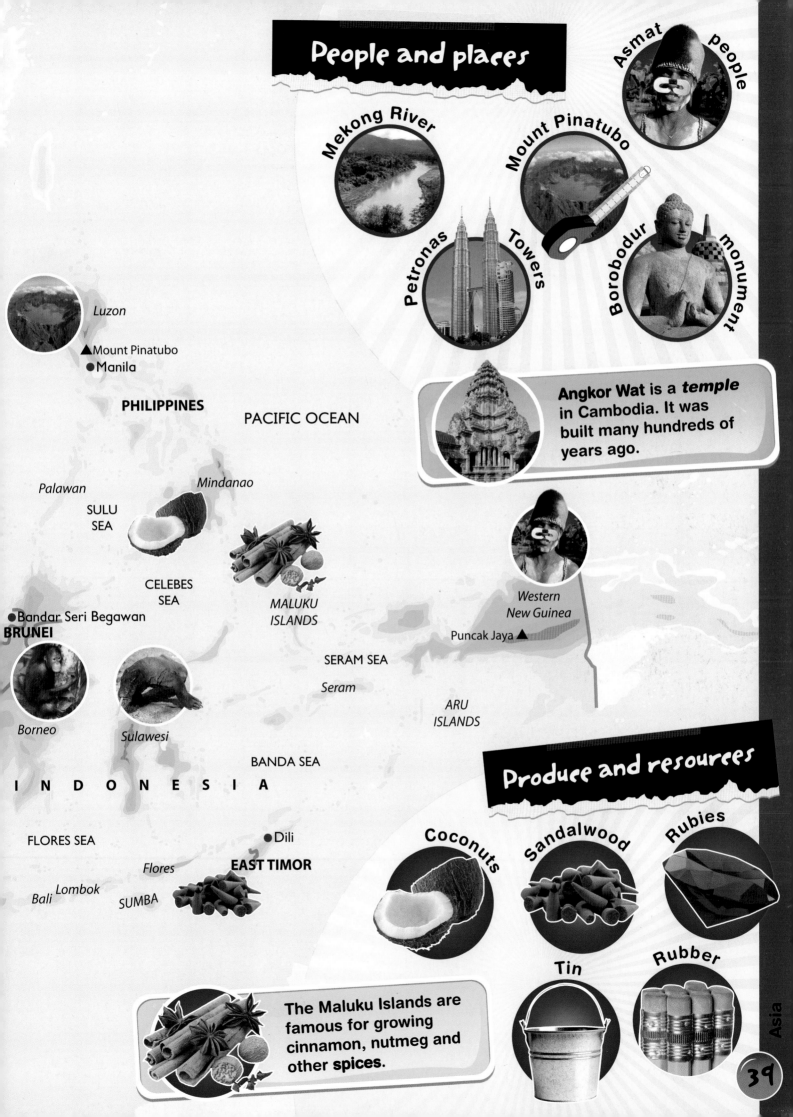

People and places

Asmat people

Mekong River

Mount Pinatubo

Petronas Towers

Borobodur monument

Angkor Wat is a *temple* in Cambodia. It was built many hundreds of years ago.

Luzon

▲Mount Pinatubo
●Manila

PHILIPPINES

PACIFIC OCEAN

Palawan

Mindanao

SULU SEA

CELEBES SEA

MALUKU ISLANDS

Western New Guinea

Puncak Jaya ▲

●Bandar Seri Begawan

BRUNEI

Borneo

Sulawesi

SERAM SEA

Seram

ARU ISLANDS

BANDA SEA

I N D O N E S I A

FLORES SEA

●Dili

Flores

EAST TIMOR

Bali *Lombok*

SUMBA

Produce and resources

Coconuts

Sandalwood

Rubies

Tin

Rubber

The Maluku Islands are famous for growing cinnamon, nutmeg and other **spices**.

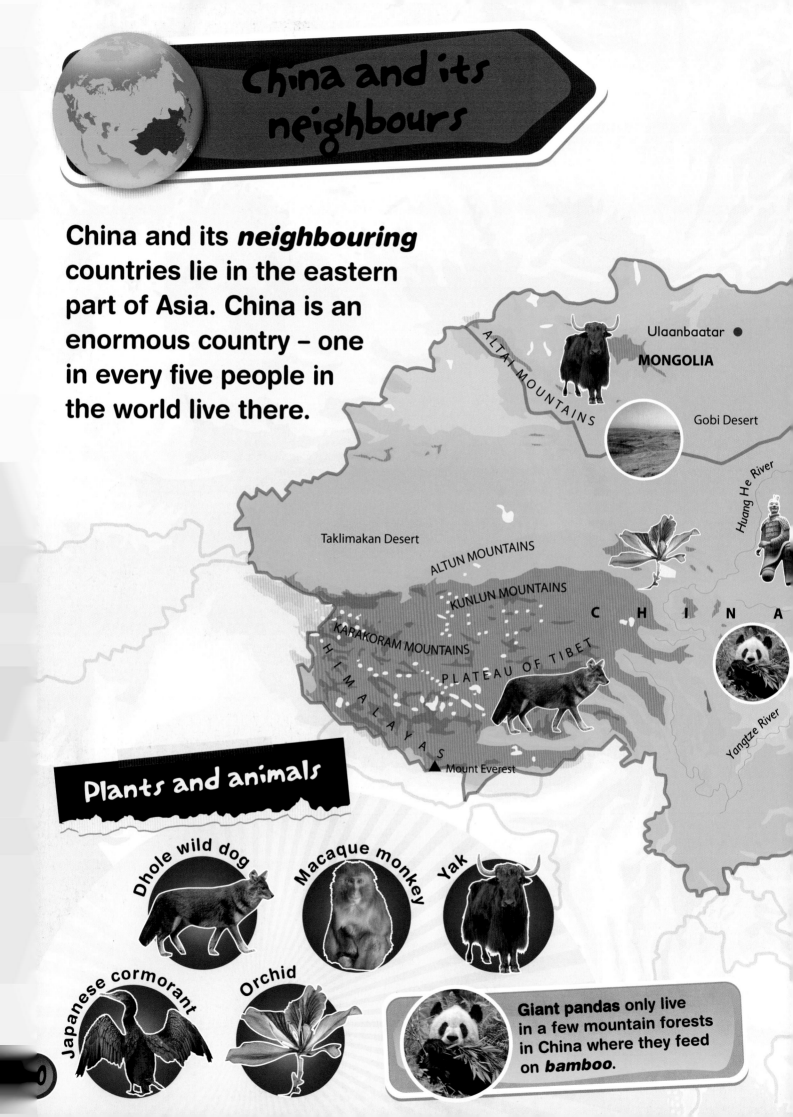

China and its neighbours

China and its **neighbouring** countries lie in the eastern part of Asia. China is an enormous country – one in every five people in the world live there.

Ulaanbaatar •
MONGOLIA

Gobi Desert

Huang He River

ALTAI MOUNTAINS

Taklimakan Desert

ALTUN MOUNTAINS

KUNLUN MOUNTAINS

KARAKORAM MOUNTAINS

C H I N A

H I M A L A Y A S

PLATEAU OF TIBET

▲ Mount Everest

Yangtze River

Plants and animals

Dhole wild dog

Macaque monkey

Yak

Japanese cormorant

Orchid

Giant pandas only live in a few mountain forests in China where they feed on **bamboo**.

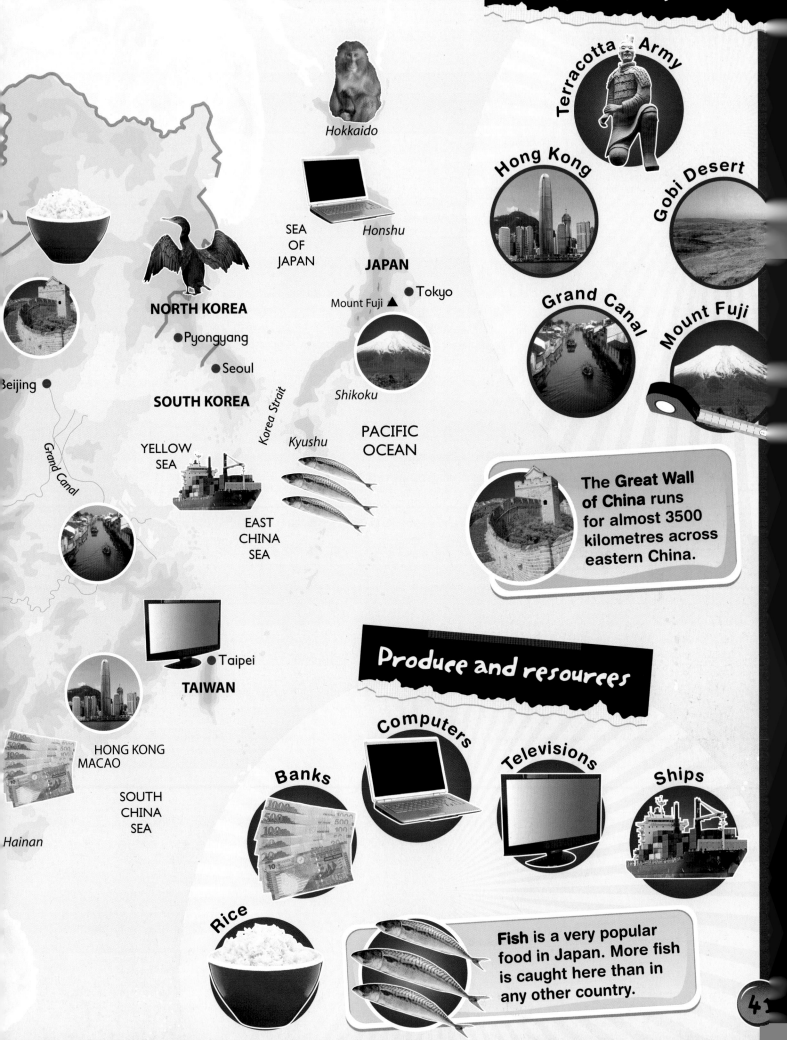

Hokkaido

SEA
OF
JAPAN

Honshu

JAPAN

● Tokyo

Mount Fuji ▲

NORTH KOREA

● Pyongyang

● Seoul

SOUTH KOREA

Korea Strait

Shikoku

Beijing ●

Grand Canal

YELLOW
SEA

Kyushu

PACIFIC
OCEAN

EAST
CHINA
SEA

Taipei

TAIWAN

HONG KONG
MACAO

SOUTH
CHINA
SEA

Hainan

Terracotta Army

Hong Kong

Gobi Desert

Grand Canal

Mount Fuji

The Great Wall of China runs for almost 3500 kilometres across eastern China.

Produce and resources

Computers

Banks

Televisions

Ships

Rice

Fish is a very popular food in Japan. More fish is caught here than in any other country.

41

Oceania

Oceania is made up of hundreds of islands in the Pacific Ocean. Oceania is the smallest continent in the world, but Australia is one of the biggest countries. New Zealand is made up of two smaller islands.

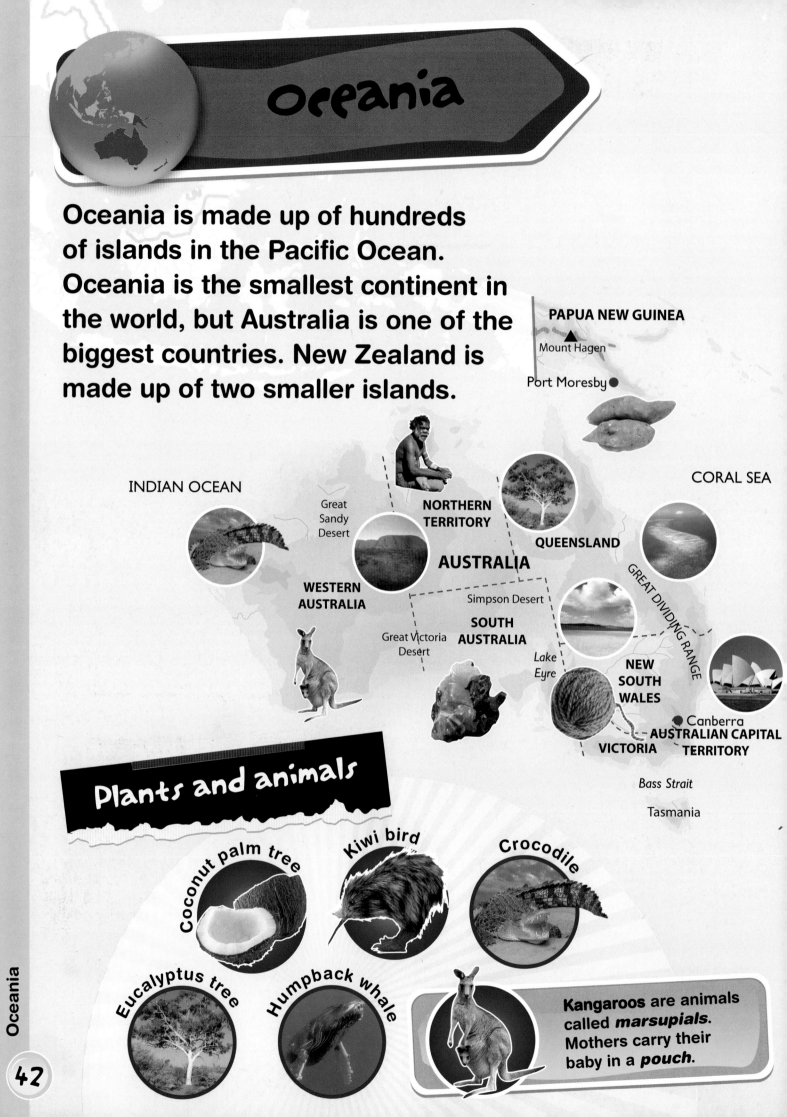

PAPUA NEW GUINEA

▲ Mount Hagen

Port Moresby ●

INDIAN OCEAN

CORAL SEA

Great Sandy Desert

NORTHERN TERRITORY

QUEENSLAND

AUSTRALIA

WESTERN AUSTRALIA

Simpson Desert

GREAT DIVIDING RANGE

SOUTH AUSTRALIA

Great Victoria Desert

Lake Eyre

NEW SOUTH WALES

● Canberra
AUSTRALIAN CAPITAL TERRITORY

VICTORIA

Bass Strait

Tasmania

Plants and animals

Coconut palm tree

Kiwi bird

Crocodile

Eucalyptus tree

Humpback whale

Kangaroos are animals called **marsupials**. Mothers carry their baby in a **pouch**.

People and places

Ayers Rock

Sydney Opera House

Aborigine people

Maori people

Lake Eyre

PACIFIC OCEAN

The **Great Barrier Reef** off eastern Australia is the longest *coral reef* in the world.

NORTHERN MARIANA ISLANDS

GUAM

MARSHALL ISLANDS

FEDERATED STATES OF MICRONESIA

Melekeok

PALAU

Palikir

Delap-Uliga-Darrit

Yaren

Bairiki

NAURU

TUVALU

KIRIBATI

SOLOMON ISLANDS

Vaiaku

TOKELAU

Honiara

WALLIS AND FUTUNA ISLANDS

SAMOA

AMERICAN SAMOA

Apia

COOK ISLANDS

VANUATU

Vila

Suva

NIUE

FRENCH POLYNESIA

NEW CALEDONIA

FIJI

TONGA

Nuku'alofa

PITCAIRN ISLANDS

North Island

Cook Strait

Wellington

NEW ZEALAND

SOUTHERN ALPS

Mount Cook

South Island

Produce and resources

Wool

Black pearls

Rugby

Opals

Sweet potatoes

New Zealand grows more **kiwi fruit** than anywhere else in the world.

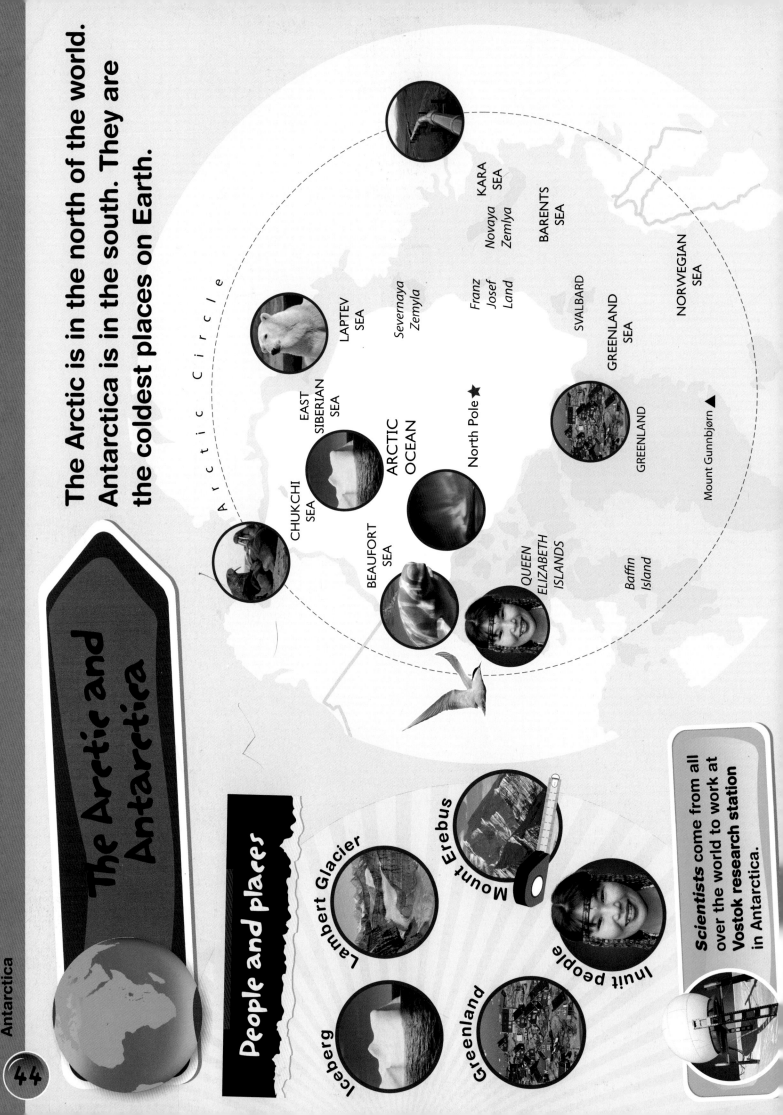

The Arctic and Antarctica

The Arctic is in the north of the world. Antarctica is in the south. They are the coldest places on Earth.

Arctic Circle

KARA SEA

Novaya Zemlya

BARENTS SEA

Franz Josef Land

NORWEGIAN SEA

SVALBARD

GREENLAND SEA

LAPTEV SEA

Severnaya Zemyla

EAST SIBERIAN SEA

North Pole ★

ARCTIC OCEAN

GREENLAND

CHUKCHI SEA

BEAUFORT SEA

Mount Gunnbjørn ▲

QUEEN ELIZABETH ISLANDS

Baffin Island

People and places

Lambert Glacier

Mount Erebus

Iceberg

Greenland

Inuit people

Scientists come from all over the world to work at **Vostok research station** in Antarctica.

44

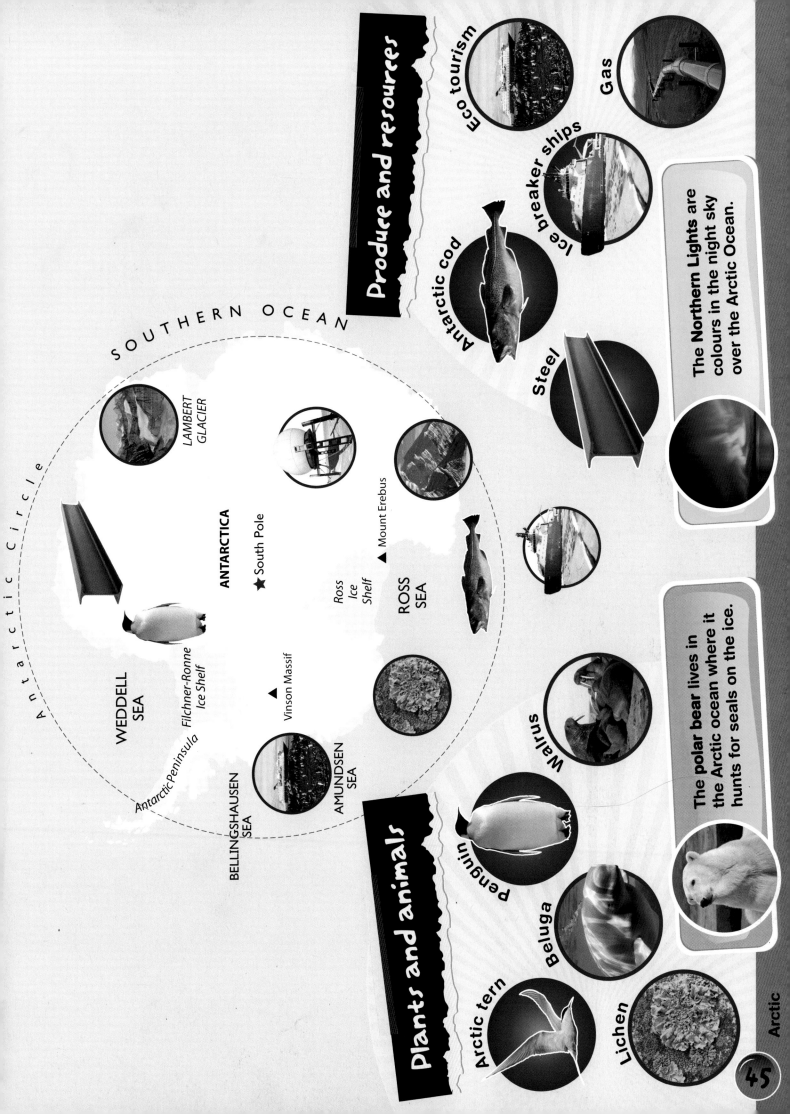

Produce and resources

Eco tourism

Gas

Ice breaker ships

Antarctic cod

Steel

SOUTHERN OCEAN

Antarctic Circle

LAMBERT GLACIER

ANTARCTICA

★ South Pole

▲ Mount Erebus

Ross Ice Shelf

ROSS SEA

WEDDELL SEA

Filchner-Ronne Ice Shelf

▲ Vinson Massif

Antarctic Peninsula

BELLINGSHAUSEN SEA

AMUNDSEN SEA

The Northern Lights are colours in the night sky over the Arctic Ocean.

The polar bear lives in the Arctic ocean where it hunts for seals on the ice.

Plants and animals

Walrus

Penguin

Beluga

Arctic tern

Lichen

Glossary

Atlas A book of maps.

Bamboo A tall grass with hard, hollow stems.

Burrow An underground home made by an animal.

Capital city The main city of a country or state.

Coastal Land near the sea.

Compass An instrument that shows which way north, south, east and west are.

Continent A large land mass. There are seven continents in the world.

Coral reef A ridge in shallow sea water made up of tiny coral animals.

Crop A plant that is grown for food.

Empress The female ruler of an empire, or group of countries or states.

Equator A line on a map that shows the middle of the Earth.

Grassland A large area of land that is mainly covered in grass.

Industry The production of a large amount of something, such as machinery.

Mainland The main area of land that makes up a country or continent.

Marsupial An animal that carries its babies around in a pocket of skin on the front of its body.

Movie studios The place where movies, or films, are made.

Neighbouring A nearby place or country.

Ocean One of the five large areas of salt water that surround the continents of the world.

Oil A liquid that is used to make machines, such as cars, work.

Pod A group of animals in the sea that live together.

Population The number of people living in a certain area, city or country.

Pouch A pocket of skin on the front of a marsupial's body that is used to carry its baby.

Rainforest A tropical area that has lots of trees that grow closely together.

Region A large area of a country.

Rink A surface of ice made for ice skating or ice hockey.

Safari A special trip to see wild animals, normally in Africa.

Scale A way of measuring the size of something, for example, a mountain.

Scented oil An oil made from something with a pleasant smell, such as roses.

Scientist A person who studies sciences such as chemistry, physics and biology to learn about the world around us.

Symbol A picture or sign that has a particular meaning.

Temple A building where people go to pray.

Textiles Woven cloth that is made in large amounts.

Tomb A place where a dead person is buried.

Tourist Someone who is visiting a country or place for pleasure.

Valley A low area of land that sits between two higher areas of land.

Vineyard Land where grapes are grown.

Volcanic The land, ash or lava that is related to a volcano. For example, Hawaii is made up of volcanic islands.

Wildlife Animals and plants.

Index